The
Graves of Academe

BOOKS BY RICHARD MITCHELL

Less Than Words Can Say
The Graves of Academe

The
GRAVES
of
ACADEME

by

RICHARD MITCHELL

LITTLE, BROWN AND COMPANY   BOSTON–TORONTO

Second Printing

Library of Congress Cataloging in Publication Data
Mitchell, Richard.
    The graves of academe.

        1. Public schools—United States—History.
    2. Educational psychology. 3. Education, Secondary—
    United States. I. Title.
    LA212.M53   371'.01'0973   81–8436
    ISBN 0–316–57508–9   AACR2

BP

Designed by Janis Capone

*Published simultaneously in Canada
by Little, Brown & Company (Canada) Limited*

PRINTED IN THE UNITED STATES OF AMERICA

*It is ordained in the eternal constitution of things
that men of intemperate minds cannot be free;
their passions forge their fetters.*

EDMUND BURKE

Foreword

This book started out to be a large collection of pieces from *The Underground Grammarian*, a dissident if tiny journal that has achieved notoriety if not fame, and to which I am a party. Such a collection was proposed by a publisher (not, I am happy to say, *my* publisher) and recommended as a not-too-difficult task. My own publisher, Little, Brown, although wise enough not to suggest such a venture, was nevertheless not as prudent when it came to signing a contract.

I spent several months choosing, ordering, and contemplating selections from *The Underground Grammarian*, intending to sort them by themes and stitch them together with running commentaries, elaborations, and second thoughts. Even third thoughts. It turned out a stupid and pointless exercise. If there is anyone who thinks that the world needs such a collection, let him make it.

What stopped me was this: As I went through scores of essays on the relation of language to the work of the mind and critical commentaries on displays of ignorance and stupidity in the written work of academicians, I could see that some were more important than others. They suggested a single theme. They were all more or less about the same thing, that special and unmistakable kind of mendacious babble that characterizes *not* politicians or businessmen, not Pentagon spokesmen or commercial hucksters, but, always and only, those members of the academic community who are pleased to call themselves the "professionals" of education. Those pieces, taken together, seemed to me at least a skimpy outline, or, better, scattered reference points suggesting something much larger and more momentous than a mere collection of ponderous inanities. It seemed to me that I could, from certain of those small articles, make out the murky form of the hidden monster whose mere projections they were, breaking here and there the oily surface of some dark pool.

As a result, I abandoned the collection and undertook the task of describing, by extrapolation from one visible protuberance to another, and with a little probing, the great invisible hulk of the beast, the brooding monstrosity of American educationism, the immense, mindless brute that by now troubles the waters of all, *all* that is done in our land in the supposed cause of "education," since when, as you see, I can rarely bring myself to write that word without quotation marks, or even fashion a sentence less than nine or ten lines long, lest I inadvertently fail to suggest the creature's awesome dimensions and seemingly endless tentacular complexities. I will try to do better. The somber subject requires clarity.

Thou canst not, however, draw out this Leviathan with an hook either. A complete, thoughtful history and analysis of American educationism would require several fat volumes, and even the author's best friends would not read it.

It is, after all, a boring subject. I have done my best to make it interesting by dwelling on its startling and horrifying attributes, which are, in any case, the most important indicators of its harmful powers. It's not a pretty sight. I have been, too, as brief as possible. In consequence, there is probably no understanding in this book of which it is not possible to say: "Well, true, but there's more to it than that." Quite so. I hope that many will someday look for the "more," but I will be content, for now, with the "true." I have everywhere provided as true an understanding as I can discover, and I am persuaded that a comprehensive and detailed historical analysis will, if it ever appears, show that my assessment of American educationism is encyclopaedically incomplete but right anyway. The prodigious monster is down there, I know, and even if its tentacles and appendages, its gross organs and protrusions, its subtle convolutions and recesses, are invisible, I have still seen enough to know the nature of the beast.

The
Graves of Academe

Propositions
Three and Seven

In the country of the blind, the one-eyed man is, as we all know, king. And across the way, in the country of the witless, the half-wit is king. And why not? It's only natural, and considering the circumstances, not really a bad system. We do the best we can.

But it is a system with some unhappy consequences. The one-eyed man knows that he could never be king in the land of the two-eyed, and the half-wit knows that he would be small potatoes indeed in a land where most people had all or most of their wits about them. These rulers, therefore, will be inordinately selective about their social programs, which will be designed not only to protect against the rise of the witful and the sighted, but, just as important, to ensure a never-failing supply of the witless and utterly blind. Even to the half-wit and the one-eyed man, it is clear that other half-wits and one-eyed men are potential competitors and supplanters, and they invert the ancient tale in which an anxious tyrant kept watch against a one-sandaled stranger by keeping watch against wanderers with both eyes and operating minds. Uneasy lies the head.

Unfortunately, most people are born with two eyes and even the propensity to think. If nothing is done about this, chaos, obviously, threatens the land. Even worse, unemployment threatens the one-eyed man and the half-wit. However, since they do in fact rule, those potentates have not much to fear, for they can command the construction and perpetuation of a state-supported and legally enforced system for the early detection and obliteration of antisocial traits, and thus arrange that witfulness and 20–20 vision will trouble the land as little as possible. The system is called "education."

Such is our case. Nor should that surprise anyone. Like living creatures, institutions intend primarily to live and do whatever else they do only to that end. Unlike some living creatures, however, who do in fact occasionally decide that there is something even more to be prized than their own survival, institutions are never capable of altruism, heroism, or even self-denial. If you imagine that they are, if, for instance, you fancy that the welfare system or the Federal Reserve exists and labors for "the good of the people," then you can be sure that the minions of the one-eyed man and the half-wit are pleased with you.

Furthermore, any institution that still stands must, by that very fact, be successful. When we say, as we seem to more and more these days, that education in America is "failing," it is because we don't understand the institution. It is, in fact, succeeding enormously. It grows daily, hourly, in power and wealth, and that precisely *because* of our accusations of failure. The more we complain against it, the more it can lay claim to *our* power and wealth, in the name of curing those ills of which we complain. And, in our special case, in a land ostensibly committed to individual freedom and rights, it can and does make the ultimate claim — to be, that is, the free, universal system of public education that alone can raise up to a free land citizens who will understand and love and defend individual freedom and rights. Like any politician, the institution of education claims direct descent in apostolic succession from the Founding Fathers.

Jefferson was in favor of education, indubitably, but he meant the condition, not the word. He held that there was no expectation, "in a state of civilization," that we could be both free and ignorant. The modifier is important; it is to suggest that we might indeed be "free" and ignorant in savagery. Free at least from the conventional and mutually admitted restraints to which civilized people bind themselves.

Using Jefferson's terms, we can derive exactly eight propositions to think about:

1. We can be ignorant and free in savagery.
2. We can be ignorant and free in civilization.
3. We can be ignorant and unfree in civilization.
4. We can be ignorant and unfree in savagery.
5. We can be educated and free in savagery.
6. We can be educated and free in civilization.
7. We can be educated and unfree in civilization.
8. We can be educated and unfree in savagery.

Jefferson asserts that the second is impossible, thereby implying the possibility of the first and the sixth. The fifth and the eighth seem unlikely, for if we are indeed educated it will be both a result of civilization and a cause of civilization. The fourth is just a quibble, for the "freedom" at issue is not freedom from natural exigencies, to which all are subject, but from the devised constraints possible only in a state of civilization. The truth of the third and the seventh, unhappily, is recommended by knowledge and experience.

Omitting those propositions that seem impossible or meaningless, we are left with:

1. We can be ignorant and free in savagery.
3. We can be ignorant and unfree in civilization.
6. We can be educated and free in civilization.
7. We can be educated and unfree in civilization.

And, of those four, Propositions 1 and 6 are explicitly Jefferson's, while 3 and 7 are *implicitly* Jefferson's. They describe conditions not only perfectly possible but perfectly real. Unfreedom, the forced submission to constraints beyond those mutually admitted by knowing and willing members of a civilization, is not unheard of. Indeed, it is, in greater or less degree, the current condition of all humanity.

Civilization is itself an institution and has, like all institutions, one paramount goal, its own perpetuation. It was Jefferson's dream that that civilization could best perpetuate itself in which the citizens were "educated," whatever he meant by that, and we do have some clue as to what he meant. He wrote of the "informed discretion" of the people as the only acceptable depository of power in a republic. He knew very well that the people might be neither informed nor discreet, that is, able to make fine distinctions, but held that the remedy for that was not to be sought in depriving the people of their proper power but in better informing their discretion.

And to what end were the people to exercise the power of their informed discretion? The answer, of course, shouldn't be surprising, but, because we have been taught to confuse government and its institutions with civilization in general, it often is. Jefferson saw the informed discretion of the people as one of those checks and balances for which our constitutional democracy is justly famous, for it was only with such a power that the people could defend themselves *against* government and its institutions. "The functionaries of *every* government," wrote Jefferson, although the italics are mine, "have propensities to command *at will* the liberty and property of their constituents." Jefferson knew — isn't this the unique genius of American constitutionalism? — that government was a dangerous master and a treacherous servant and that the first concern of free people was to keep their government on a leash, a pretty short one at that.

Consider again Propositions 3 and 7: 3. We can be ignorant and unfree in civilization, and 7. We can be educated and unfree in civilization. Imagine that you are one of those functionaries of government in whom there has grown, it seems inescapable, the propensity to command, in however oblique a fashion and for whatever supposedly good purpose, the liberty and property of your constituents. Which would you prefer, educated constituents or ignorant ones? Wait. Be sure to answer the question in Jefferson's terms. Which would you rather face, even considering your own conviction that the cause in which you want to command liberty and property is just — citizens *with* or *without* the power of informed discretion? Citizens having that power will require of you a laborious and detailed justification of your intentions and expectations and may, even having that, adduce other information and exercise further discretion to the contrary of your propensities. On the other hand, the ill-informed and undiscriminating can easily be persuaded by the recitation of popular slogans and the appeal to self-interest, however spurious. It is only informed discretion that can detect such maneuvers.

And that's how government works. There is nothing evil about it. It's perfectly natural. You and I would do it the same way. In fact, the chances are good that we *are* doing things that way, since more and more of us are in fact functionaries of government in one way or another and dependent for our daily bread on some share of the property of our constituents, and sometimes (as in the public schools) upon the restriction of their liberty.

It was the genius of Jefferson to see that free people would rarely have to defend their freedom against principalities and powers and satanic enemies of the good, but that they *would* have to defend it daily against the perfectly natural and inevitable propensities of functionaries. Any fool can see, eventually, the danger to freedom in a self-confessed military dictatorship, but it takes informed discretion to see the same danger in bland bureaucracies made up entirely of decent people who are just doing their jobs. But Jefferson was optimistic. As to the liberty and property of the people, he saw that "there is no safe deposit for them but with the people themselves; nor can they be safe with them without information." And he was convinced, alas, that the people could easily come by that information: "Where the press is free, and every man able to read, all is secure."

That sounds so simple. A free press, and universal literacy. We have those things, don't we? So all is secure, no? No.

Just as we cannot assume that what we call "education" is the same as Jefferson's "informed discretion," we cannot assume that Jefferson meant what we mean by "press" and "able to read." In our time, the press, in spite of threats real or imagined, is in fact free. And, if we define "literacy" in a very special and limited way, almost everyone is able to read, more or less. But when Jefferson looked at "the press," what did he see? Or, more to the point, what did he *not* see? He did not see monthly periodicals devoted entirely to such things as hair care and motorcycling and the imagined intimate details of the lives of television stars and rock singers. He did not see a sports page, a fashion page, a household hints column, or an astrological forecast. He did not see a never-ending succession of breathless articles on low-budget decorating for the executive couple in the big city, career enhancement through creative haberdashery, and the achievement of orgasm through enlightened self-interest. He did not see a nationwide portrayal of "the important" as composed primarily of the doings and undoings of entertainers, athletes, politicians, and criminals.

He would not, I think, have been unduly dismayed by all that. Of course, he would have been *dismayed*, but not unduly. Such things are implicit in the freedom of the press, and if enough people want them, they'll have them. (Jefferson would surely have wondered *why* so many people wanted such things, but that's not to the point just now.) Jefferson did, naturally, see "the press" giving news and information, but, more than that, he also saw in it the very *practice* of informed discretion. In his time, after all, *Common Sense* and *The Federalist* papers were simply parts of "the press." And "every man able to read" would have been, for Jefferson, every man able to read, weigh, and consider things like *Common Sense* and *The Federalist* papers. He would have recognized at once our editorial pages and our journals of enquiry and opinion, but he would have found it ominous that hardly anyone reads those things, and positively portentous that this omission arises not so much from casual neglect as from a common and measurable *inability* to read such things with either comprehension or pleasure.

Thus Jefferson is cheated. The press is free and almost everyone can make out many words, but all is not secure. Wait. That's not quite clear. Some things *are* secure. The agencies and institutions of government are secure. The functionaries whose propensity it is to command our liberty and property, they are secure. And, as the one-eyed man is the more secure in proportion to the number of citizens he can blind, our functionaries are the more secure in proportion to those of us who are strangers to the powers of informed discretion. It is possible, of course, to keep educated people unfree in a state of civilization, but it's much easier to keep ignorant people unfree in a state of civilization. And it is easiest of all if you can convince the ignorant that they *are* educated, for you can thus make them collaborators in your disposition of their liberty and property. That is the institutionally assigned task, for all that it may be invisible to those who perform it, of American public education.

Public education does its work superbly, almost perfectly. It works in fairly strict accordance with its own implicit theory of "education," an elaborate ideology of which only some small details are generally known to the public. This is hardly surprising, for the rare citizen who actually *wants* to know something about educationistic theory, a dismal subject, finds that it is habitually expressed in tangled, ungrammatical jargon, penetrable, when it is at all, only to one who has nothing better to do. I hope, little by little, to dissect and elucidate that theory, for it is in fact even more frightening than it is dismal. For now, I can take only a first but essential step and urge you to consider this principle: The clouded language of educational theory is an evolved, protective adaptation that hinders thought and understanding. As such, it is no more the result of conscious intention than the markings of a moth. But it works. Thus, those who give themselves to the presumed study and the presumptuous promulgation of educational theory are usually both deceivers *and* deceived. The murky language where their minds habitually dwell at once unminds them and gives them the power to unmind others.

We will, with appropriate examples, explore the evolution of that strange trait, especially in that portion of the educational establishment where it is most evident: that is, among the people to whom we have given the training of teachers and the formulation of educational theory. In the cumbersome and complicated contraption we call "public education," the trainers of teachers have special powers and privileges. Although in law they are governed by civilian boards and legislatures, they are in fact but little governed, for they have convinced the boards and legislatures that only teacher-trainers can judge the work of teacher-trainers. That wasn't hard to do, for boards and legislatures are made up largely of people who have, in their time, already been blinded by the one-eyed man, having been given, as helpless children, what we call "education" rather than practice in informed discretion. The very language in which the teacher-trainers explain their labors will quickly discourage close scrutiny in even a thoughtful board member, perhaps *especially* in a thoughtful board member, who has after all, other and more important (he thinks) things to do.

It is not strictly true that the public schools are a state-supported monopoly. There are other schools. But the teacher-trainers are certainly a state-supported monopoly. There are no other teacher-trainers than the ones we have, and they are all in the business of teaching something they call "education." No one knows exactly what that is, and even among educationists there is some mild contention as to whether there actually exists some body of knowledge that can be called "education" as separate from other knowable subjects. You may want to make up your own mind as to that, for in later chapters you will see examples of what is actually done by those who teach "education." But for now we must consider the usually unnoticed effects of the monopoly they enjoy.

The laws of supply and demand work in the academic world just as they do in the marketplace, which is to say, of course, that what is natural and reasonable will not happen where government intervenes. Our schools can be usefully likened to a nationalized industrial system in which the production of goods is directed not by entrepreneurs looking to profit but by social planners intending to change the world. Thus it is the business of the schools, and the special task of the educationists who produce teachers, to generate both supply *and* demand, so that the nation will want exactly what it is they intend to provide.

Within the academic marketplace, there are many enterprises other than educationism, however. Historically, they have not seen themselves in competition with one another, although I'm sure that the faculties of the medieval universities were not reluctant to claim that *their* disciplines were more noble than the others. Individual professors, of course, must indeed have competed for students, by whom they were paid, but the students, many of whom were to become professors themselves, were free to devote themselves to whatever discipline seemed good. But between one discipline and another there seems to have been, rather than competition, sectarianism.

A similar sectarianism has been revivified by our current educational disorders. If you ask a professor of geography why we seem to be turning into a nation of ignorant rabble, he will not be able to refrain from pointing out that we don't teach geography anymore and that high school graduates aren't even sure of the name of the next state, never mind the climatic characteristics of the Great Plains or the rivers that drain the Ohio Valley. Professors of physics will allude to the all-too-inevitable consequences of ignorance of the laws of motion and thermodynamics. You can easily devise for yourself the comments of professors of mathematics, languages, history, literature, and indeed of any who teach those things we think of as traditional academic disciplines. Their views will be, of course, at least partly predictable expressions of self-interest; however, they will also be correct, and, if taken all together, will indeed tell us much about our present troubles.

The academic world is like any other group of related enterprises in which everybody can provide something but nobody can provide everything. For the building of houses, for instance, we need many different things, and they are not easily interchangeable. When we need copper tubing, we need copper tubing, and we can't make do with wallboard instead. If houses are built, therefore, many people making many different things will be able to produce what is both useful and profitable. And, while the makers of copper tubing won't have to worry about competition from the makers of wallboard, they will have to be mindful of other makers of copper tubing and also of the makers of plastic tubing. That will be good for the whole enterprise.

Suppose, though, that the copper-tubing people should, through quirk or cunning, secure for themselves some special legal privilege. First they persuade the state, which already has the power to license the building of houses, to prohibit the use of plastic tubing. That's good, but so long as the state is willing to go that far, the copper-tubing makers seek and achieve a regulation requiring some absolute minimum quantity of copper tubing in every new house. Now you must suppose that the copper-tubing lobby has grown so rich and powerful that the law now requires that fifty percent of the mass of every new house must be made up of copper tubing.

Houses could still be built. Walls, floors, and ceilings could be made of coils and bundles of copper tubing smeared over with plaster or stucco. Copper tubing could be cleverly welded and twisted into everything from doorknobs to windowsills and produced in large sizes for heating ducts and chimneys. The houses would be dreadful, of course, and, should you ask why, you will discover that craftsmen in the building trades are more direct and outspoken than college professors. They'll just tell you straight out that these are lousy houses because of all that damn copper tubing. If the professor of mathematics were equally frank, he'd tell you that our schools are full of supposed teachers of mathematics who have studied "education" when they should have studied mathematics.

This is, I admit, not an exact analogy. The manufacture of copper tubing actually does have some relationship to the building of houses, while the study of "education" has no relationship at all to the making of educated people. The analogy would perhaps have been better had I chosen, instead of the manufacturers of copper tubing, the manufacturers of gelatin desserts. To grasp the true nature of the place of educationism in the academic world, you have to imagine that houses are to be made mostly of Jell-O — each flavor equally represented — and that the builders must eat a bowl an hour.

(Well, that analogy fails, too. Jell-O is at least a colorful and entertaining treat with no known harmful side effects. The same cannot be said of the study of "education.")

Our public system of education, from Head Start to the graduate schools of the state universities, might also be called a government system. Those who teach in its primary and secondary schools are required by law to serve time, often as much as one half of their undergraduate program, in the classes of the teacher-trainers. Should they seek graduate degrees, which will bring them automatic raises, they will still have to spend about one half their time taking yet again courses devoted to things like interpersonal relations and the appreciation of alternative remediation enhancements. The educationistic monopoly is strong enough that in at least one state (there are probably others, but I'm afraid to find out), a high school mathematics teacher who is arrogant enough to take a master's degree in mathematics will discover that he is no longer certified to teach that subject. If he wants to keep his job, he must take a degree in "mathematics education," which will, of course, permit him to spend *some* of his time studying his subject. Even where there is no such visibly monopolistic requirement, the laws and regulations of the public schools, which have been devised by educationists in the teachers' colleges, provide an effective equivalent.

The intellectual climate of the public schools, which must inevitably become the intellectual climate of the nation, does not seem to be conducive to the spread of what Jefferson called informed discretion. The intellectual climate of the nation today *came* from the public schools, where almost every one of us was schooled in the work of the mind. We are a people who imagine that we are weighing important issues when we exchange generalizations and well-known opinions. We decide how to vote or what to buy according to whim or fancied self-interest, either of which is easily engendered in us by the manipulation of language, which we have neither the will nor the ability to analyze. We believe that we can reach conclusions without having the faintest idea of the difference between inferences and statements of fact, often without any suspicions that there are such things and that they *are* different. We are easily persuaded and repersuaded by what seems authoritative, without any notion of those attributes and abilities that characterize authority. We do not notice elementary fallacies in logic; it doesn't even occur to us to look for them; few of us are even aware that such things exist. We make no regular distinctions between those kinds of things that can be known and objectively verified and those that can only be believed or not. Nor are we likely to examine, when we believe or not, the induced predispositions that may make us do the one or the other. We are easy prey.

That these seem to be the traits of the human condition always and everywhere is not to the point. They just won't do for a free society. Jefferson and his friends made a revolution against ignorance and unreason, which would preclude freedom in any form of government whatsoever. If we cannot make ourselves a knowledgeable and thoughtful people — those are the requisites of informed discretion — then we cannot be free. But our revolutionists did at least provide us with that form of government which, unlike others, does grant the possibility of freedom, provided, of course, the public has the habit of informed discretion. That possibility is all we have just now.

Proposition 3 is in effect. We are largely a nation of ill-informed and casually thoughtless captives. Even when we are well-informed and thoughful, however, we cannot be free where the character of the nation and its institutions must reflect the ignorance and unreason of the popular will. But if we *are* well-informed and thoughtful, we can take comfort in the fact that our form of government is carefully designed to preclude that condition described in Proposition 7. As long as we remain a constitutional republic, we cannot ever be both educated and unfree. It just won't work, and that may be the single greatest insight of the makers of our revolution.

Therefore, whatever it is they do in the teachers' colleges of America has had and will always have tremendous consequences. By comparison with the attitudes and intellectual habits and ideological predispositions inculcated in American teachers, the acts of Congress are trivial. Indeed, the latter proceed from the former. If, as a result of the labors of our educationists, we were obviously clear-sighted and thoughtful and thus able to enjoy the freedom promised in our constitutional system, then we would know something about those educationists. If, on the other hand, we are blind and witless, then we would know — if there are any of us who *can* know — something else about them. To know anything at all about those educationists, however, we must look at what they do, at what they *say* they do, and even at *how* they say what they do.

The
End of the String

As a schoolboy, I always presumed that my teachers were experts in the subjects that they taught. My physics teacher must, of course, be a physicist, and my history teacher a historian. I knew that my music teacher was a musician, for I had actually heard him play, and, during a dismal year in military school, I could see with my own eyes that the Professor of Military Science and Tactics was a bird colonel.

Even when I became a schoolteacher myself, quite by accident, I imagined that I had been chosen for the work because of my knowledge of the subject I was to teach. It turned out not to be exactly so, for I was soon asked to teach something else, of which my knowledge was scanty. No matter, I was told. I could bone up over the summer. Eventually, I was asked to teach something about which I knew nothing, nothing at all. Still no matter. I seemed to be a fairly effective teacher and at least smart enough to stay a lesson or two ahead of the students. That's just what I did. No one saw anything wrong with that, and the students never caught me. It was nevertheless depressing, for it led me to suspect that my physics teacher perhaps hadn't been a physicist after all.

What then, *exactly*, was he? What was it that made a teacher a teacher, if it wasn't, as it obviously wasn't, an expert knowledge of some subject matter? How could it be that I was able to teach, to the complete satisfaction of my colleagues and supervisors, and with no *visible* detriment to my students, a subject of which I knew practically nothing at first, and of which, after a year of teaching it, I knew just about what anyone could know of it after one year of study? Was there something *wrong* with that? Was there something wrong with me that I suspected that there *was* something wrong with that?

It took me many years to find answers to those questions, and, when I did, it wasn't because I was looking for them. It was because I finally settled in what was called a State Teachers College. (Like Pikes Peak, it had no apostrophe.) As it happens, it is no longer a State Teachers College. The legislature later enacted a long and complicated law which had, as far as I can tell, the sole effect of removing from that title the word "Teachers." The college has not changed much, except that where it was once unashamedly a teachers' college, it is now ashamedly a teachers' college. There I was, and I couldn't help looking around.

At the end of my first semester, I walked into a classroom where I was to give a final examination. (We don't do much of that anymore, since it may just be a violation of someone's rights.) On the blackboard was the final examination that had just been given to some other class. Very neatly written it was, too. The last question — I'll never forget it — was worth fifty-two percent of the grade: "Draw all the letters of the alphabet, both upper and lower case." Draw.

There is some truth in the "ivory tower" notion of academic life. I had spent my whole life in one school or another, and I was, of course, faintly aware that I was only faintly aware of what was going on out in the world. When I looked at that blackboard and imagined all those students dutifully "drawing" the alphabet in their blue-books, I realized that I didn't even know what was going on down at the other end of the hall. Nevertheless, it still didn't occur to me that this astonishing examination had something to do with those questions that I had long since stopped asking myself.

It turned out, of course, that what I had seen was a final examination in one of those "education" courses, about which, at that time, I knew nothing. Well, that's not quite true: I did know one thing, because earlier that semester I had looked into a classroom where something amazing was happening. There, in front of the class, stood an unusually attractive young lady, a student, tricked out in a fetching bunny outfit — not the kind you're probably imagining, just a pair of paper ears pinned into her hair and a stunning puff of absorbent cotton somehow or other tacked on behind — and clothes, too, of course, but I can't recall any details. She was reading aloud, with expression, and even with an occasional hop, from a large book spread out flat at about hip level, glancing down at it remarkably infrequently. Large type. She was doing a practice lesson. I awarded her instantly an A plus.

So I knew two things about the making of a teacher. Both seemed engaging rather than repellent. After all, who can be against legible writing on the blackboard? To be sure, I myself wouldn't have assigned it a value of more than half the grade on a final examination; perhaps, had it been in my charge to foster, I would simply have required it as a tool of the trade without bestowing upon it any special credit at all. And it did occur to me that what the students drew in their examination books might not be an accurate measure of their skill in drawing the same things on a blackboard, an unusually intractable medium, but the *motive* seemed good. And as for pretty girls in cunning outfits, what could be more cheering? It seemed to me that those teacher-trainers must be amiable and playful folk with well-developed aesthetic sensibilities and a penchant for drama, in bold contrast to the rest of us who taught what you call "subjects," dour and narrow people reciting lectures and devising "thought" questions. And who knows? Could it be that I would now actually remember the political consequences of Henry's sad pilgrimage to Canossa if only my history professor had put on sackcloth and lectured on his knees?

And I began to watch the teacher-trainers in idle moments, in *my* idle moments, that is, not theirs. They were rarely idle. They were busy rumbling down the hall pushing metal carts laden with projectors and loudspeakers, which they actually knew how to hook up and operate. I could hear them in the next classroom shoving the desks into sociable circles so that, as in King Arthur's court, no one would be disadvantaged by having to sit below the salt, or breaking up into small groups, so that understanding could be reached by democratic consensus rather than imposed by authority. Sometimes whole classes could be heard singing — a delightful change of atmosphere in precincts otherwise darkened by realism and naturalism and the intellectual despair of eminent Victorians.

All in all, I thought the teacher-trainers harmless and

childlike, optimistic and ingenuous. I knew, to be sure, that many of them held what they called doctorates in things like comparative storage systems for badminton supplies and for cafeteria management, but so what? They weren't pretending to teach anything that called for traditional training in scholarship, were they? Doctorates in education, I remembered from my days in graduate school, are much easier to get than any other kind, but what did that matter? A doctorate, after all, was just a union card, a ticket of admission to a remarkably good life, and why shouldn't those decent and well-meaning people have doctorates just like everybody else? As to whether what they did had any value in the training of teachers, I just didn't know. I wasn't curious enough to pay thoughtful attention, and they didn't seem to be hurting anyone. Live and let live.

So I did. Once the novelty of their techniques wore off, and long before it dawned on me that those techniques were better called "antics," I just stopped thinking about them. The teacher-trainers were not in my mind at all when I started to publish *The Underground Grammarian* in 1976. The Bicentennial Year was in my mind, and Tom Paine and even William Lloyd Garrison, and, most of all, the ghastly, fractured, ignorant English that is routinely written and spread around by college administrators, the people charged with the making and executing of policy in the cause of higher education in America. I presumed that those administrators would be the natural prey of a journal devoted to the display of ignorance in unlikely places. It never even struck me then that most administrators were once the teacher-trainers who were not in my mind.

And I will beg your indulgence, reader, in suggesting that when you look at the world and wonder what's going on, the teacher-trainers are not in your mind. Nuclear weapons and taxes are in your mind, along with politicians and other criminals. Pollution and racial discord are in your mind. Prices double and pleasures dwindle, violence and ignorance multiply and expectations diminish, and all the season's new television shows are aimed at demented children, and master sergeants have to puzzle out in comic-book style manuals how to pull the triggers on their Titan missiles, and sometimes, in a moment of pure panic, you wonder whether you shouldn't have voted for Goldwater after all. And when you wave a finger this way and that, trying to point it at someone, anyone, the teacher-trainers are not in your mind.

Sometimes, to be sure, you do suspect and even indict "the schools." Ah, if only "the schools" would do this or that. But what? Everybody has a formula, sort of. Money, obviously, isn't the answer. They have money beyond counting. Less money can hardly be the answer — just ask the National Education Association. So what are we to do? Public schools? Private schools? Vouchers? Integration? Remediation? Consolidation? Back to basics? Forward to relevancy in bold innovative thrusts?

Then again, you may not even ask these questions, for to do so is to see a connection that not many Americans have thought to make. Millions of us have nothing at all to do with the schools. We have no children in the schools, and we don't know what they're doing, and we don't much care, except about the taxes we pay to support the enterprise. We can easily think of many things that must be far more important than education, a notably dreary topic in any case. Surely politics is more important than education. So is economics. Technology. National defense. Even art! And the six o'clock news in any city in the land makes it perfectly clear that the most important things that happened in your part of the world today were murders, rapes, and a fire of unknown origin in an abandoned warehouse. And as for the schools, most of us just hope that they'll teach the children to read and write and cipher someday soon and just not bother us. We have all those important things to worry about and we really can't be bothered with wondering about whether the schools should experiment with a ground-breaking return to the self-contained classroom.

In fact, the destiny of this land, of any land, is exactly and inevitably determined by the nature and abilities of the children now in school. The future simply has no other resources. And, an even more dismaying fact, because it tells of *us*, not them, this land as it is today is the exact and inevitable result of the nature and abilities of the schoolchildren that *we* were. And the things that you think important, everything from the politics to the rapes and murders and fires, are what they are and have for us the meanings that they have precisely because of what we were.

Public education, because it is so nearly universal and because, notwithstanding minor variations, it is a monolithic and self-sustaining institution, has more power to create our national character than anything else in America. While it does not bring us oil shortages or volcanic eruptions, it does determine what we will think and do about such things. It determines what we will feel and how we will do the work of the mind. This should not be surprising. You, and you alone, could do as much if you could somehow manage to influence almost every American child day after day for about twelve years, although, as an individual controlling consciousness, you would probably do a better job in many respects. There is, of course, no individual controlling consciousness in the institution of education — no villain need be — but the institution, like any institution, has a kind of mind and will of its own. It changes, if at all, only very slowly, and, since *you* don't find it as important as politics or fire, it changes only at the will of those relatively few people who actually do find it important, because they live by it. Nor is it their will — and why should it be? — to make any change that is not in their self-interest. "They," of course, are a loosely confederated host of administrators, bureaucrats, consultants, professors, researchers, and Heaven only knows how many other titled functionaries. They are a very diverse group, but they have, with astonishingly rare exceptions, one thing in common. They have all been through the process that we call teacher-training, and most of them have done some of that themselves. They are the people who are not in your mind when you wonder what the hell is happening to us.

And they would never have gotten back into my mind had I not undertaken, for what I now think frivolous reasons, what turned out to be a serious and infuriating study of the use of language, a study that had to lead to a consideration of the *meaning* of the use of language. That study is, of course, the business of *The Underground Grammarian*, which has been accurately enough described as a journal of radical, academic terrorism. It is radical because it seeks in language the root of the thoughtlessness that more and more seems to characterize our culture. It is academic both because the tenor of the study to which it subjects the work of its victims is scholastic and because it finds the most egregious examples of mindless and mendacious babble neither in the corporation nor in the Congress but in the schools. It is terrorist because it exploits the fear that many academics feel when they know that their words might appear in print before the eyes of the public, mere civilians who are not members of the education club.

Here is the brief statement of editorial policies that appeared in the first issue of *The Underground Grammarian*:

 ## Editorial Policies

The Underground Grammarian is an unauthorized journal devoted to the protection of the Mother Tongue at Glassboro State College. Our language *can* be written and even spoken correctly, even beautifully. We do not demand beauty, but bad English cannot be excused or tolerated in a college. *The Underground Grammarian* will expose and ridicule examples of jargon, faulty syntax, redundancy, needless neologism, and any other kind of outrage against English.

Clear language engenders clear thought, and clear thought is the most important benefit of education. We are neither peddlers nor politicians that we should prosper by that use of language which carries the least meaning. We cannot honorably accept the wages, confidence, or licensure of the citizens who employ us as we darken counsel by words without understanding.

My first motives were just about what you would expect from an English teacher: a supposed reverence for that "Mother Tongue," the noble and ancient language of Shakespeare and Milton and all the others; the notion that the judicious choice of a semicolon was a nice display of what Veblen called "the instinct of workmanship," a good thing; and especially that sense of smug satisfaction that comes from knowing exactly why to use the word "nice" when making a nice display. There was also the natural, and perfectly justifiable, contempt that any front-line teacher feels for administrators. So many of them seem to be born aluminum-siding salesmen who took a wrong turn somewhere along the line. Nor is that contempt mitigated by the fact that many of them (but by no means all) were once front-line teachers themselves. On the contrary, that reveals what they really think of teaching: a humble and tedious calling useful only as a necessary step to a better life and better pay. There is furthermore, in almost every teacher, a small, dark current of fascism, and the work of administration not only permits but actually encourages it.

I did say, to be sure, that "clear language engenders clear thought, and clear thought is the most important benefit of education," but that was little more than a recitation. That's what we're expected to say in this business, and we keep saying it and nodding, saying it and nodding. And, like most of the things that people are expected to say, it's true in a way, and false in a way, and not well thought out. There is an important principle to be drawn here: Many of our supposed "ideas" are in fact recitations, recitations not of what we think or understand but of what we simply believe that we believe. Thinking is done in language, and understanding, a result of thinking, is expressed in language, but, when we simply adopt and recite what has been expressed, we have committed neither thinking nor understanding. When the first issue of *The Underground*

Grammarian appeared, I had neither thought about nor understood that lofty proposition about clear language and clear thought. But the words were there on the page, and they demanded attention.

All that talk about the ability to write letters of application for jobs is bunk; here is the real value of teaching everybody, *everybody*, to write clear, coherent, and more or less conventional prose: The words we write demand far more attention than those we speak. The habit of writing exposes us to that demand, and skill in writing makes us able to pay logical and thoughtful attention. Having done that, we can come to understand what before we could only recite. We may find it bunk or wisdom, but, while we had better reject the bunk, we can accept the wisdom as truly our own rather than some random suggestion of popular belief. If we have neither the habit nor the skill of writing, however, we have to guess which is the bunk and which the wisdom, and we will almost invariably guess according to something we feel, not according to something to which we have given thoughtful attention.

I had not, in fact, given thoughtful attention to "clear thought" and "clear language" and the ways in which they might relate to each other, but I had at least taken hold of one end of what turned out to be a long and tangled string. An examination, if only of comma faults and dangling participles, had begun. Examination has a life of its own. You simply cannot think about commas and the place of modifiers without finding that you are thinking about thinking. It is impossible to examine language at any level without examining the work of a mind. I knew that Wittgenstein had said that all philosophy was the examination of language, but I assumed, because I wasn't paying thoughtful attention, that he was referring to the obvious fact that philosophy was about ideas, and that ideas could be read only in language. I don't think that anymore. I'm convinced that he was talking about language *as* language, with its commas and modifiers, and especially about writing, a special case of language, permanently accessible.

Consider, for example, the following sentence, which was quoted without comment in a much later issue:

Teratology

> During the 1980–81 school year, the project will provide teachers and administrators with education and support designed to optimize the behaviors and conditions in the school which support student learning to the extent that at least two thirds of the teachers receiving training and support in Expectations will report, on a specifically designed survey, changes in at least two school related operational characteristics that have been identified as critical elements of the network of expectations that support learning.

What we learn from studying that sentence has very little to do with the digest of rules in the back of the composition handbook. It has to do with the nature of a mind and the way it does its work. That is revealing enough, but it's only the beginning. The mind we see at work in that sentence is not the mind of an isolated eccentric. That writer is a member, and probably in all too good standing, of a community of minds and the inheritor of a massive tradition. It represents what is obviously acceptable to a society of like-minded peers and superiors and subordinates. It speaks, one might say, for *the* mind of a vast bureaucracy, and, furthermore, since no mind works that way naturally, it must have *learned* that trick.

When we study that sentence, therefore, we study the intellectual climate of the society in which such work of the mind is not only acceptable but desirable, and we study the traditions and practices that must have formed both the society and the individual mind. That example is in no way extraordinary or even unusual; it is, in fact, typical. (You will know that, of course, if you have any acquaintance with the business of the schools, and, if you haven't, you'll soon see for yourself.) So we can ask: What *is* the intellectual climate of that society? What traditions and practices have formed that climate? Having answers to those questions, we can ask: Why is a society so endowed and so constituted given the task of teaching minds to work well, and how likely is it to succeed in that work?

In speaking of that "society" in such general terms, I have to advise civilians that I do not mean "the teachers," or at least not simply the teachers. Most people think that teachers *are* the agents of public education and that all those guidance counselors and curriculum facilitators and others are merely support services. This is not so. Of all the agents of our system of public education, the teachers are by far the least influential, and what they actually accomplish or don't accomplish in their classrooms has very little to do with the worth of "education" in the large sense. This is not to say that teachers are uninfluenced by the intellectual climate of the system as a whole, far from it, but only that they are the lowliest foot-sloggers in a vast army. Some of them will rise from the ranks and will be no longer teachers. They will become the people whose minds work like the mind of that writer just cited. Indeed, if their minds work that way, they are all the more likely to rise. But as long as they remain teachers they are, and they're so treated as, mere employees, who may or may not be seeking admittance to the seats of power.

Incipient schoolteachers — I have known hundreds of them — are generally decent young people of average intelligence. Some are stupid, of course, and some rarer few are brilliant. Almost all of them seem a bit more than ordinarily ethical, and I can't believe that any one of them ever decided to be a teacher for the sake of doing harm. Furthermore, the task of teaching a mind to work well is not a particularly difficult one. Teachers do not have to be brilliant, although they probably shouldn't be stupid. In short, almost all of those who seek to be teachers are quite capable of being good teachers, but something happens to them on the way to the classroom. They fall into bad company. Here is an example of what they must face:

Pontiffs and Peasants

Unlike socialism, the realm of educationism was never meant to be a classless society. Just now it's an emasculated feudalism whose few surviving *pugnantes* have decided to settle down with the unholy but happy Saracens, leaving the miserable *laborantes* to fend for themselves under the silly governance of the puffed-up *orantes*. The go-getter, self-promoting grant-grabbers have all wangled themselves cushy consultancies and juicy jobs in government. The wretched tillers of the soil are hoeing hard rows in the public schools and risking life and limb in the cause of minimum competence. The jargon-besotted clergy are bestowing upon each other rich benefices of experiential continua and peddling cheap remediational indulgences, fighting to keep their teacher-training academies growing in an age of closing schools and dwindling faith in bold innovative thrusts in non-cognitive curriculum design facilitation. Fat flocks, fat shepherds. Things do look bad, but let us not despair. The Black Death has been reported in Arizona, and it may yet spread.

It's not always easy to tell the pontiffs from the peasants. The sumptuary laws no longer apply. In the time of love-beads, both classes wear love-beads; in the time of Levi's, Levi's. Our best clue — *always* the best clue when we want to assess the work of the mind — is the language used by each class, *Lumpensprache* by the peasants and *Pfaffesprache,* a classier lingo indeed, by the pontiffs.

Here's a typical passage of the latter as it appeared, unfortunately without attribution, in an otherwise splendid column by Howard Hurwitz, a syndicated writer on education:

> These instructional approaches are perhaps best conceived on a systems model, where instructional variables (input factors) are mediated by factors of students' existing cognitive structure (organizational properties of the learner's immediately relevant concepts in the particular subject field); and by personal predispositions and tolerance toward the requirements of inference, abstraction, and impulse control, all prerequisite to achievement in the discovery or the hypothetical learning mode.

So. It may mean that what a student learns depends on what he already knows and on whether or not he gives a damn. For a pontiff of educationism, that's already a novel and arresting idea, but if he said it in plain English he wouldn't be allowed to teach any courses in it. Indeed, if he *could* say it in plain English he would probably have enough sense not to say it, thus disclosing to the world that years of study have brought him at last to a firm grasp on the obvious.

Even when intoning the obvious, however, a pontiff keeps his head down. Did you notice that "perhaps"? He doesn't actually commit himself to the proposition that approaches are best conceived as a model where variables are mediated by factors; he is willing only to opine that approaches are "perhaps" best conceived as a model where variables are mediated by factors. If that were humility rather than self-defense, it would suit him well, for he seems to think that "conceived" means "understood" and that "mediated" means "mitigated" and that "factors" and "variables" can mean anything at all. He's not so good with semicolons either.

That point is important. Although inflated with fake erudition, *Pfaffesprache* always reveals, inadvertently, its roots in the vulgar, but usually honest, *Lumpensprache*. Thus we find in that passage the defensive errors of the ignorant, who always use too many modifiers and achieve thereby either redundancy or incoherence. There is no need to specify that a student's "disposition" is "personal" or to elaborate "subject" into "the particular subject field." We are not enlightened by hearing that a property is organizational or that the relevant is immediately relevant. "The hypothetical learning mode" tells us only that this pontiff is hazy about the meanings of "mode" and "hypothetical" and short on "learning."

The pontiff, of course, preaches what he practices in some teacher-training academy. Nevertheless, in spite of his baleful influence, many of his students do not adopt his ignorant babble. They cling faithfully to their own ignorant babble.

They become schoolteachers and compose "thought" questions for study guides: "What did the sculpture told the archologists?" They admonish parents: "Scott is dropping in his studies he acts as if don't care. Scott want pass in his assignment at all, he had a poem to learn and he fell to do it." When asked to demonstrate their own literacy, they go out on strike, demanding on the placards "quality educacion" and "descent wages."

Maybe you *can't* fool all of the people all of the time, but the pontiffs can fool all of the peasants forever. That accounts for the fact that the society of educationism is made up of two apparently dissimilar classes. Deep down where it really counts, they're equally less than minimally competent.

We can understand why the educationists defend so truculently that bizarre article of their faith which pronounces superior intelligence and academic accomplishment traits not suitable to schoolteachers. Well, they may have a good point there. There's more than enough violence in the schools already. If we were to send a bunch of bright and able students to study with the hypothetical learning mode pontiff, they'd ride him out of town on a rail and hurry back to burn down the whole damn teacher-training academy.

It seems, at first, a puzzling fact that those who have spent as much as one half of their time in college studying under professors who fancy that they conceive their instructional approaches on systems models mediated by factors can then go out into the world unable to compose complete sentences or even to spell "education." However, not until quite recently, and then only in response to external demands, have the teacher-trainers thought it their responsibility to see to it that newly graduated teachers could in fact write complete sentences and spell correctly. (We will see later some entertaining examples of what they *do* in response to those demands.) Those things were the business of the English department people, and if they failed to teach them, well, too bad, the fledgling teachers would just have to do without them.

Furthermore, the students in teacher-training academies

are not in fact expected to adopt or even to examine the language of that "mediated by factors" passage. That is the language of the education textbooks, not the language of the classroom, although in education courses whole classes are not infrequently devoted to the reading of some text, as mealtime in monasteries is devoted to Scripture. Should a student ask, for instance, the *meaning* of the passage cited, he would probably be told something very much like the suggested translation. Should he ask, however, why such an obvious generalization had to be couched in such strange language, I don't know what answer he would get, but I would bet that he will soon want to reconsider his choice of a calling. Should he take the last step and ask why anyone would think such a banal truism worthy of serious study, then he probably won't have to reconsider his choice of a calling. His adviser will do that for him.

The passage is only a ritual recitation which is not supposed to be subjected to thoughtful scrutiny. It is a formulized pastiche of acceptable jargon terms and stock phrases. While it has, for the inattentive, a formidable sound, it is the kind of writing that is surprisingly easy to compose for anyone who is familiar with all of its traditional devices. (The craft of making such prose, strangely enough, is similar to what we can find to this day in the extemporaneous epic recitations of mendicant storytellers in the marketplaces of the Near East. They remember and stitch together thousands of recurring epithets, stock descriptions of the hero, his horse, his armor, standardized metaphors and narrative devices. Educationistic prose, however, is usually less stirring than the recitations of clever beggars.) And who, in any case, would *want* to scrutinize such a passage? Who? A more than ordinarily inquisitive (and perhaps skeptical) student, that's who. One who might indeed be able to compose a complete sentence and even spell "education."

Even in teacher-training academies, there are such students. They usually learn to keep their mouths shut, but those who don't can be a nuisance. They are not only disconcerting in class, but they are likely to give the place a bad name by complaining in public that their education courses seem silly. (Most schoolteachers — go and ask some — will shrug off their education courses as a kind of necessary evil, a "waste of time." Those courses, however, are a "waste of time" only for the students enrolled in them; for the institution of teacher-training they are immensely profitable.) That is why the pontiffs feel most comfortable when they can in fact preach to peasants, which is one of the reasons (there are others) for that "bizarre article of faith."

The ordinary civilian, who may very well remember with awe the apparent erudition of some teacher or other, is not generally aware of this strange doctrine, but there is little enthusiasm in the teacher-training business for outstanding intellectual accomplishment in would-be teachers. One claimed theory is that since a teacher must be able to "relate" to the students before any learning can happen, the teacher ought to be as much like the student as possible, very unlikely in the case of an especially intellectual teacher. The democratizing leaven of ignorance, therefore, may be in fact desirable in a teacher. It is also a supposition of educationistic folklore that intellectuals are likely to be more interested in the subjects they teach than in their students, which will make them cold and distant, perhaps even authoritarian. The latter, at least, is hard to quarrel with, for the pronouncements of one who can in fact speak with authority on some subject are by definition "authoritarian." They are also, however, exactly the pronouncements any thoughtful person would want to hear if he sought knowledge. This doctrine would seem to suggest that if you feel the need of a diet it would be better to consult with a hairdresser than with a physician, for the hairdresser is much easier to relate to than the frosty physician, whose advice, furthermore, would surely be authoritarian.

The tangled evolution of this strange tenet, which is not at all the same as the contention that it doesn't require more than ordinary intelligence to teach children the work of the mind, will be considered in later chapters. For now, though, we have to consider the problem that it causes for those who hold it. One part of that problem is invisible to the believers: How can we at once denigrate the authoritarianism of the intellectual while adopting in our own pronouncements the tone, if not the substance, of authoritative intellectualism? While that question does not trouble the teacher-trainers, who are simply unmindful of it, it must bother us, eventually. That part of the problem *visible* to them, probably because it is a matter of clear self-interest, is this: If intellectualism is undesirable, its opposite must be desirable; but the opposite of intellectualism, by whatever name, is hard to champion in a supposedly academic context. It would take a bold professor indeed to come out in favor of ignorance and stupidity and offer in their favor arguments based on knowledge and reason, arguments of the sort that are still expected in some of our colleges and universities. It requires only a presumptuous professor to plump for ignorance and stupidity on other grounds, and this is not unheard of, especially in enthusiasts of drugs and pop pseudo-religions. For the institution of teacher-training as a whole, however, something more publicly defensible is needed, and, since the defense can afford neither kookiness nor the appeal to knowledge and reason, it must rest upon what is likely to prove emotionally acceptable to the largest possible audience.

And there is such a defense. Over and against the overweening demands of scholarly intellectualism, the teacher-trainers have set the presumably unquestionable virtues of what they call "humanism." They use this term in so many different contexts and to characterize so many different kinds of acts and ideologies that I will not attempt to discuss it fully here. It will just have to grow on you. It does not, as you might think, denote as usual a particular school of thought or slant of philosophical or religious speculation connected especially but not exclusively with the Renaissance, although many who use the term *have* heard of the Renaissance. This is something closer to "humaneness," as that word is used by what used to be called the "Humane Society," an organization that publicly deplored the cruel treatment of horses. One of the aims of "humanistic" educationism is to deplore the cruel treatment of children subjected to the overbearing demands of knowledge, scholarship, and logic by the traditional powers of authoritarian intellectualism.

We will return to that strange "humanism," for it is one of the two fundamental principles that can be said to make up the underlying theory of education in America. The other is what might be called the iron law of behavior modification. Like Free Will and The Omniscience of God, educationistic humanism and behavior modification are ultimately irreconcilable, and their collisions are at the heart of our educational disorders. The theologians, at least, are not unaware of their stubborn little problem, but the educationists seem oblivious to the contradictions inherent in their two favorite principles. Nor could they abandon either, for in their "humanism" they can pose as philosophers and priests, and as modifiers of behavior they can claim to be scientists and healers. We can consider their claims by looking first at the roots of the presumed science of educationism.

The
Wundter of It All

The true grandfather of modern educationism is neither Horace Mann, who has a bit more to answer for than we usually imagine, nor John Dewey, who in fact has less to answer for than you would conclude from the deeds of people who haven't read him. Mann had very good intentions, and if he was unable to predict the future of state-supported education in an age of ballooning statism, he was hardly alone. Dewey's thought was so complicated and diverse, and often so muddily expressed, that it is not (much) to his discredit that facile faddists have seized slogans from his books and elaborated them into strange pedagogical practices.

The illuminating spirit, or evil genius, of modern educationism was Wilhelm Max Wundt, a Hegelian psychologist who established the world's first laboratory for psychological experimentation at the University of Leipzig, where he worked and taught from 1875 to 1920. He dreamed of transforming psychology, a notably "soft" science dealing in vague generalizations and abstract pronouncements, into a "hard" science, like physics. About human behavior, he hoped to make exact and publicly verifiable statements of empirical fact, from which he could go on to do what scientists must do, formulate hypotheses and make predictions subject to the test of observation and experiment.

Those are hardly evil designs, and they are, of course, as Hegel might have warned Wundt had he had the chance, clearly an expression of the *Zeitgeist* of the late nineteenth century. They are not evil any more than science itself is evil, but their "scientific" intentions take on a strange flavor when we consider that *Zeitgeist*. That was the age in which Zola embarked on a mighty series of novels, an enterprise that he fancied a genuinely scientific experiment. That's the point of his now-forgotten book on the novel as a kind of science, *Le Roman Experimental*: True, we cannot raise whole generations in miniature worlds in the laboratory and chart their deeds and destinies, but we can, if we are sufficiently knowledgeable and disciplined, do pretty much the same thing in a book. Zola, thus, was never without his notebook, in which he jotted, probably to the consternation of all who knew him, his "observations" of (presumably) unguarded human behavior.

That was also the age of Marx and Freud, and the growing suspicion, the worm that late Victorian intellectuals were bound and determined to eat even if it *didn't* kill them, that Darwin had shown us only one of the mighty determinisms that governed human behavior and destiny. Who can blame Wundt, therefore, if he imagined that one who knew enough could measure, predict, and even elicit all those things that we call feelings, sentiments, emotions, attitudes, and ideas, to say nothing of mere deeds. But while we are considerately not blaming him, let us call on his own "science" in a rough and ready way, without precise measurements, alas, and be a little suspicious of his motives.

People who make their livings in "soft" sciences and the arts are not entirely at ease in the company of chemists and physicists and other "hard" scientists. In such company, the psychologists and sociologists and the professors of English feel like touch-football enthusiasts who have wandered by mistake into the locker room of the Pittsburgh Steelers. Only true philosophers, not professors of philosophy, are entirely immune to that nasty suspicion that rises in the heart of the "humanist" when he hears about recombinant DNA or quarks. (Well, that's not quite true. The untempered clod is also immune, a fact whose importance will appear later.) This is a modern condition, and quite unlike that of older times, in which the fledgling "hard" scientists were held in contempt by those who did their work entirely in the mind without the help of apparatus, proper only to artisans. It seems only fair; it's the alchemist's revenge.

Wundt, with his laboratory and machines, was certainly trying to better himself and win for his discipline a new kind of legitimacy. It was just for that reason that he attracted so many students, many of them Americans who came home to found schools of educational psychology and psychological testing and to impress upon our whole system of schooling the indelible mark of clinical practice. One of them was a certain James Cattell, who, while playing with some of Wundt's apparatus, made a remarkable and portentous discovery. Here, in brief, is the story, as told by Lance J. Klass in *The Leipzig Connection* (The Delphian Press, 1978), a useful little book on the influence of Wundt in the history of American educationism:

One series of experiments Cattell performed while at Leipzig examined the manner in which a person sees the words he is reading. By testing adults who knew how to read, Cattell "discovered" that individuals can recognize words without having to sound out the letters. From this, he reasoned that words are not read by compounding the letters, but are perceived as "total word pictures." He determined that little is gained by teaching the child his sounds and letters as the first step to being able to read. Since individuals could recognize words very rapidly, the way to teach children how to read was to show them words, and tell them what the words were. The result was the dropping of the phonic or alphabetic method of teaching reading, and its replacement by the sight-reading method in use throughout America.

The consequences of Cattell's "discovery" have surely been enormous, for they include not only the stupefaction of almost the whole of American culture but even the birth and colossal growth of a lucrative industry devoted first to assuring that children won't be able to read and then to selling an endless succession of "remedies" for that inability; but Wundt in fact brought us much worse. He brought us the very atmosphere in which such silliness can thrive. Out of the internal exigencies of his "science," he was led to consider "education" a human phenomenon similar to other human psychic conditions, a conditioned response to stimuli. "Teaching" had to be seen as the application of stimuli that will elicit whatever response we choose to call "learning." Contrariwise, anyone who has learned something, to read or cipher, for instance, must obviously have done so as a result of being exposed not simply to the *substance* of his learning, the reading or ciphering, but to some stimulus that probably, but by no means certainly, was visited upon him some-where in the vicinity of reading and ciphering.

The widespread acceptance of the teaching of reading as inspired by Cattell was possible only where there was already a predisposition to concentrate not on the substance of what can be learned but on some attribute that can be detected in the supposed learner. Exactly that predisposition was pro-vided by Wundt's view of teaching and learning as psycho-logical stimuli and responses, an arrangement presumed to have its own validity without reference to *what* was taught and learned. This view was gladly received in the United States, where, as we will see, a growing educationistic estab-lishment made up mostly of people with little or no academic expertise was looking for attractive alternatives to the con-stricting demands of "subjects."

Thus it is that our educationists prefer not to treat the multiplication table as something that just has to be learned. They rather think of multiplying as a desirable "student outcome," a "behavioral modification" of one who does not know how to multiply. This would be only a harmless play-ing with words if it weren't for the fact that not all students learn to multiply with equal ease. If we simply think of the multiplication table as a set of numbers that must be learned by brute force, we can demand more force of those who fail to learn. If we think of the ability to multiply as a "be-havioral objective," an appropriate response to stimuli, then the student who doesn't learn to multiply must drive us to seek *other* stimuli and perhaps, in stubborn cases, to decide that learning the multiplication table has only limited value for the student outcome of multiplication. From such a view, other follies may flow.

The folly at hand, the word-recognition teaching of reading, is the result of just such tormented thinking. It *is* perfectly true that people who can read do not stop to sound out letters. That, therefore, is an attribute of readers. So, to the mortally wundted, the path to reading requires the *not* sounding out of letters as a student outcome, and student behavior must be modified accordingly. Thus, the rare and pesky student who has learned the sounds of some letters must be discouraged, which stimulus will elicit a response characteristic of those who do in fact know how to read. Simple, no?

Leaving aside the incidental, if momentous, destruction of a whole nation's ability to read, we have still two far more important and ominous legacies from Wundt. We can afford to leave the reading problem aside because it is only a practice, a practice that can change, and, in fact, does show signs of changing. But the major principles that generated and maintained that practice show no signs of changing, and those principles generate and maintain numerous other unnatural practices and will yet bring us more. They can be put thus:

1. Mental and emotional conditions and events are natural phenomena subject to natural law and fully subsumable in a rigidly scientific system.

2. Teaching and learning are mental and emotional conditions and events.

In another context, of course, there would be no need to make of the second a "principle" equal in weight to the first, but here it seems useful. These principles are ominous legacies not because they are false. For all I know, and for all *anyone* knows, they may be true. But that wouldn't make them ominous either, although it certainly would lead me to drop this project, and all others, here and now. What makes them ominous is that they are utterly, for humanity in its present state at least, beyond our powers to test. They require what we seem unable to achieve, the total understanding of human beings *by* human beings. We lack that. And, for all the promises of our Freuds, Marxes, and Wundts, we seem no closer to it then ever before. We may assume what suits us, of course, about the nature of humanity, and when we act on our assumptions, consequences will flow accordingly. American educationists have assumed the truth of Wundt's principles, in spite of the fact that few of them have ever heard of Wundt, and the consequences are what we see.

It is possible to imagine — in fact, you don't have to imagine, for Marx makes a good example — some meticulously logical and disciplined thinker who, having made assumptions something like Wundt's, could derive from them an iron system, complete and internally consistent. Such might have been the nature of American education today had Wundtian psychology been adopted by expert and learned thinkers. But it was in fact adopted by the educationists, who already saw themselves as the appointed democratic supplanters of learned and expert thinkers, remnants of an elitist authoritarianism. When the principles of Wundt are taken up by people actually hostile to academic learning and traditional intellectualism, strange consequences will flow. Thus it is that educationistic thought and language have a disconcerting hermaphroditic quality, for the educationist is committed on the one hand to the proposition that human qualities are quantifiable and predictable (through the work of the intellect, presumably, for how else can we quantify and predict?), and on the other hand to the proposition that the practice of the intellect is of less significance and "value" than the possession of certain human qualities.

Here is an excerpt from *The Underground Grammarian* that shows how the automatic if unknowing adherence to Wundt's principles, in combination with the disorder of the intellect enforced by anti-intellectualism, causes things to happen in the schools and teacher academies:

 ## The Most Unkindest Cutting Edge of All

In March of 1979, we printed some gabble by a then-unidentified doctoral candidate at New Mexico State University in Las Cruces. It was about "a short extrapolation to the prediction of trans-personal innovations from self-actualization traits." Ten months later, the writer was identified as Robert D. Waterman. The man who fingered him was a colleague, James Dyke, who wanted not the handsome reward we had offered, but rather to rebuke us for our treatment of Waterman.

Having pointed out, as though it made a difference, that Waterman's degree was not in guidance but in Educational Management/Development, Dyke said further:

> I hold little faith in your critical abilities with respect to Bob Waterman until such time that you can demonstrate that you can handle the cutting edge of the exploration of ideas without bleeding.

And he even sent along an actual *piece* of the cutting edge, Waterman's complete abstract and a thin slice from Chapter II of the dissertation, "Value and Philosophical Characteristics of Transpersonal Teachers."

We admit that we have no "critical abilities with respect to

Bob Waterman," but Dyke may have meant something other than what he wrote. The critical abilities that we *do* seek are those that enable us to write *exactly* what we mean. They would also find "until such time that" a silly inflation of "until," and an example of the thoughtlessness so common in freshman compositions.

Well, no matter. Dyke doesn't claim to *be* the cutting edge. So let's take up his challenge and try to handle the edge itself. We'll start with the very *edge* of the edge, Waterman's first paragraph. Mind your fingers:

> Though an increasing interest on the part of the educational community is being shown in transpersonal teaching, the literature reflects a lack of empirically based studies concerning the teacher characteristics associated with its adoption. The purpose of this study, therefore, was to attempt to identify characteristics (values, attitudes, and teaching philosophy) pertinent to transpersonally oriented non-public school teachers and to compare and contrast those characteristics to those of public school oriented teachers.

We expected some incisiveness out there on the cutting edge, but the first paragraph is clouded by uncertainty and imprecision:

❧ Like other educationists, Waterman evades clear declarations and active verbs, as though he were afraid to take any chances even on a bland generalization like the assertion that somebody is showing interest in something. He retreats into an awkward and periphrastic jumble, saying that increasing interest "on the part" of somebody is "being" shown in transpersonal teaching. (Let's get to *that* later.)

❧ The timidity of educationistic prose is not simply a stylistic twitch. It expresses an uncertain mind and the fear of challenge. That "literature" named by Waterman either lacks something or it doesn't, but he will say only that it "reflects" a lack. Likewise, he assigns himself not exactly the task of "identifying" but only of "attempting" to identify something or other — just in case.

❧ In what way, we wonder, is a characteristic "pertinent to" some teachers different from a characteristic "of" some teachers? What can we suppose about the mind that prefers the former to the latter?

❧ Are those "public school oriented teachers" actually teachers in public schools, or could they be teachers *anywhere* who just happen to be obsessed with thinking about the public schools? Could they even be teachers who face in the direction of public schools?

Enough. The cutting edge in New Mexico is indeed blunted and ragged, and probably septic as well, and it was thoughtful of Dyke to warn us of the horrible wound it might inflict. Let's get out the long tongs.

Educationists feel secure, or as secure as they *can* feel, when they can prattle about the unmeasurable. If you natter about attitudes and values, no one can prove you a fool by pointing to some facts. However, while the retreat from the measurable provides comfort for the educationist, it makes it hard for him to claim, as he would so dearly love to, that "education" actually is a body of knowledge and that his Faculty Club card should *not* be stamped: "Valid only when accompanied by an adult." What a dilemma.

Many doctoral candidates in education just head for the nearest exit. They bestow upon us "conclusive findings" as to the efficacy of yellow traffic lines on the cafeteria floor and the number of junior high school girls in the suburbs of Duluth who elected badminton rather than archery.

For those who want to do *serious* research way out there on the cutting edge, however, a trickier dodge is needed, and the education academy is quick to supply it. Most D.Ed. programs require of their candidates no competence in foreign languages, which makes them attractive and accessible to those whose verbal abilities are meager. It assures that those abilities will *remain* meager, too, lest the teacher academies hatch out some thankless bird capable of seeing, and telling the world, that the teacher-training professors just can't make sense. The teacher-trainers, therefore, make virtue of necessity by claiming that an educationistic scholar doesn't need verbal skill anyway, but a one-semester course in statistics instead. And that's why their "research" bristles with commensurate model analyses and stepwise regression strategies.

Now we can look at Waterman's "transpersonal teaching." In the pages that we have, there is no definition, but we know that

> the personal characteristics related to transpersonal teaching are: (1) a view of man as essentially and inherently good at his core, (2) that the locus of power and authority in one's life is within the individual, and (3) that when dealing with life situations it is most effective to apply one's values to a solution with flexibility, and free of preconceptions or prejudice.

We already know how Waterman writes, so we're not surprised by redundancy or jargon, or even that disconcerting violation of parallelism. What does surprise us is that the work of the mind way out there on the cutting edge of the exploration of ideas sounds so much like a mimeographed prospectus for a non-denominational Sunday school class to be taught by some amiable but slightly addled addict of popular self-help paperbacks and magazine articles about the cutting edge of the exploration of ideas in Marin County.

Waterman's values, quasi-theological and pseudo-philosophical, can become objects of "research" only to educationists. First they circulate questionnaires, either homemade or, as in Waterman's case, prefabricated by other educationists. Then they tabulate the "answers," which are usually spaces filled in or numbers checked by captives eager to finish a stupid questionnaire. The answers reveal, of course, only what the answerers have chosen to say, which may or may not reveal what they feel or believe. In fact, it probably does not, especially in this "research." Even *non*transpersonal teachers know enough not to give straight answers to prying busybodies.

Most of us can see a difference between a study of angels and a study of testimony about angels. Waterman sees that the R^2 of Self-Regard is .0123, and, of Inner-Directed, a hefty .4544. Existentiality's R^2 is a modest .0460. Yeah. And next year he's going to whip off Weltschmerz and Ennui, and we'll know *exactly* how we feel about the cutting edge of the exploration of ideas in New Mexico.

In the meantime, though, we are going to cook up a little "empirically based study" of our own. We're just dying to find out some nifty data about the R^2 of Hubris.

It would surely be an injustice to Wundt, who was meticulously intelligent, by all accounts, to think that *he* would be a party to the granting of a doctorate, even in Educational Management/Development, for such cloudy work. Nevertheless, he asked for it. The presumed method of Waterman's "empirically based study" promises to quantify mental and emotional conditions and events in publicly verifiable measurements. Those strange numbers, left unexplained in the original article, are typical of the measurements. They are determined statistically by counting up and manipulating the answers to the questionnaires. Such is the educationist's equivalent of the scientific method, and even Wundt would reject it.

There is no counting the doctorates in education that have been awarded to those who have done nothing more than tabulate the answers to questionnaires. That such degrees are so common, however, is not only because the work is easy, bad enough, but also because the supposed objects of study often cannot be known directly. When they can, in fact, they are obviously trivial. When all the badminton and archery coaches have sent in their completed questionnaires, then you know something about the junior high school girls in the suburbs of Duluth. Or, to be more exact, you know what the badminton and archery coaches *say* about those girls. Nevertheless, the *nature* of the knowledge is such that it is publicly verifiable through direct observation. But it is of very limited use and will not bring great renown to its discoverer.

On the other hand, the nature of knowledge about the "values, attitudes, and teaching philosophy" of "transpersonal teachers" does not recommend such knowledge as verifiable through observation. We do not "see" such things; we can only make inferences about them. We do not even know what "transpersonal" might mean, for its form, analogous to "transcontinental," suggests nothing rational. Nor can we figure it out by imagining its antonym, i.e., what would we mean if we said that some teacher was "nontranspersonal." When we are *told* the "personal characteristics related to transpersonal teaching," we learn only that teachers who seem to have these certain beliefs rather than others are being *called* "transpersonal," but the term distinguishes them only from the nontranspersonal teachers, who, presumably, do *not* have those beliefs. And a surly pack of misanthropes and defeatists *they* must be.

Never mind. Educationists love to sound technical, and they have a penchant for giving important-sounding names to things that need no names at all. In that fashion, for instance, they do not call a very small class a very small class or helping one student helping one student. They decide that such things are properly named "micro-teaching." It may seem to you that it doesn't make any difference, but it turns out to make a big difference indeed. You cannot write dissertations and articles, you cannot teach courses in teacher academies, you cannot get grants of public money, you cannot hire out as a consultant, you cannot set up a project and assemble a staff, if all you're going to do is talk about very small classes and the fact that a teacher will often help one student. You *can* do all of those things, and more, if you are an expert in micro-teaching. Thus Waterman, by giving a classy name to people who would otherwise be nothing more than reasonably kind, confident, and resourceful teachers, provides himself with a topic worthy of serious study.

Well, nice people are nice, no doubt. But how do we *know* that, and how can we decide which are the *nicer* nice people and by precisely how much they are nicer? This is the kind of concern that modern educationism has inherited from Wundt's by now much-debased principles. And answers are sought not by recourse to evidence but by the gathering of testimony, testimony invariably and inevitably tainted by subjectivity. It would be bad enough that such methods nullify the value of educationistic "research." What is far worse is that such research becomes the pattern for the study of "education" generally. Students of teacher-training are continuously exposed to such presumed methods of inquiry. Since they spend so much of their time in education courses, they can have little training in rigidly scientific disciplines, even if they intend to teach them, and they are easily bamboozled into thinking that this kind of exercise is science. Their bewilderment has to be compounded by the fact that this putative science is about things which, for other purposes than dissertations, educationists will claim as human "values" to be inculcated as *separate* from "mere" intellectual attainments. Those are things like Waterman's Self-Regard, Existentiality, and Inner-Directed (which desperately needs a substantive).

The educationistic mind is deeply divided against itself. It wants to follow Wundt and believe that teaching and learning are objectively measurable phenomena and that those who study teaching and learning are therefore scientists and worthy of chairs in colleges and universities. At the same time it wants to contend that the profoundly important results of an education, especially the education of a teacher, are attitudes, values, and "philosophies" that transcend cognition. Waterman, an educationist, asks this kind of question: How do public and private school teachers compare with each other in their Existentiality? He who asks after the degree of your Existentiality may just as well ask for a numerical value for your hunger, and will, in either case, simply have to accept what you tell him. Such "research" wouldn't even make an interesting parlor game.

But what else can Waterman, or any orthodox educationist, do? He is not likely to ask, for instance: How do public and private school teachers of mathematics compare with each other in their knowledge of mathematics? That question could be answered in publicly verifiable measurements. But it is not an answer that a prudent educationist would want, and it would probably not win you a doctorate in any graduate school of education in America. Your committee will throw you out for several reasons: Since the teaching of *anything* is the design and application of appropriate stimuli, the teacher's *knowledge* of mathematics, although there ought to be some, is *not* what makes him a teacher. We do not teach mathematics just so that students can *do* mathematics, but for a higher purpose, for the inculcation, perhaps, of an appreciation of Logic and Rationality; so you would be better to seek findings about Logic/Rationality Appreciation, which is exactly as easy to measure as Existentiality. Your research is, in any case, likely to give a false impression, since many private school teachers, to the detriment of their professionalism, are not legitimately certified and have probably taken more courses in mathematics than in education, which makes their possibly superior knowledge of mathematics a matter of no consequence.

In other words: Measurable things are not important; unmeasurable things are paramount. Let us therefore measure only the unmeasurable. Of course, Wundt never dreamed of measuring the unmeasurable. He claimed rather that the psychological conditions and events of humanity were not unmeasurable at all, and that the task of psychological science was to discover *how* to measure them. He did not suggest that we go around asking people how they felt, however, for reasons that are perfectly obvious to anyone with any rudimentary understanding of science. But he did hold, for equally obvious reasons, that the study of human psychology required the direct observation of human beings. That tenet of Wundtianism, hardly startling, has been happily accepted by educationists, for if there is one thing they have always at hand it is a large collection of captive human beings.

You have surely heard of "child-centered" education, that process that will educate the "whole child." It sounds so decent. What could be better than centering on the child, the whole child, no less? But what, exactly, do half-baked neo-Wundtians mean when they speak of "child-centered" education? Here is an article that provides some evidence toward an answer to that question:

The Nonredundant Interactive Relationship of Perceived Teacher Directiveness and Student Personological Variables to Grades and Satisfaction

Recent research has shown that a number of student variables — authoritarianism, dogmatism, intelligence, conceptual level, convergent-divergent ability, locus of control, anxiety, compulsivity, need for achievement, achievement orientation, independence-dependence, and extraversion-introversion — may moderate the relationship between teacher directiveness and grades and satisfaction. There is a fair degree of moderate intercorrelation among these student variables and such intercorrelation suggests that some of the found interactive relationships may be overlapping or redundant. The purpose of the present research is to develop multivariate mathematical models of the interactive relationships using stepwise regression strategies. Such models should facilitate a more parsimonious interpretation of the interactive relationships which are . . .

We were going to show you *all* of that mess and even give you the name and address of the chappie who made it, but we can't. Before our typesetter was able to finish, a member of our staff borrowed the original (and only) copy and took it to Texas. There, while fumbling for his entry permit at the Immigration Control Office, he lost the evidence. Maybe it's just as well. There's no telling what those Rangers might have done had they caught him with a smoking dissertation abstract. They don't cotton much to that kind of stuff down there.

We *can* tell you, at least, that the original came from Calgary, Alberta, and we have to hope, if justice is ever to be done, that the Mounties don't want any of this stuff in their country either. They shouldn't have much trouble getting their man — *and* his sidekick — in this case. The author and his dissertation adviser were so proud of themselves that they had their photographs printed right on the page with the evidence. Perfectly decent and respectable young fellows they seemed, too. Who would have thought it?

Since personology must be too subtle a science for the likes of us, we cannot explain how "personological" variables might be different from differences in persons. We would guess, though, that "student" variables are young variables studying to become teacher variables. And we're a little disappointed by that list of student variables, a measly twelve items. In the better teacher academies, you'd never get a doctorate for such a skimpy, or "parsimonious," elaboration of the obvious commingled with the incomprehensible.

The most instructive thing about the passage is that its pretentiousness is eloquently, although inadvertently, undone by its timidity. Notice that all those nifty variables *may* "moderate the relationship." Educationists won't take chances, even on the obvious and simple. After all, how can we be sure, without multivariate mathematical models of the interactive relationships, that different people feel different about different things?

Of course, should this research achieve its goal, we might have to change our opinions. A "parsimonious interpretation" of a "fair" degree of "moderate" intercorrelation is not to be sneezed at. Before such an awesome discovery, we'd just have to back off, treading cautiously in our best stepwise regression strategies.

 ———————————————————————————————

Let's try to imagine some possible facts and events that might incite such an undertaking, that is, the development of multivariate mathematical models of interactive relationships. First, be careful to remember something that might easily blow away in the storm of jargon — all of this has something to do with children in school. So we can imagine: There are some children in school. They are, in some ways, different from each other, that is, they have (could that be the right word?) different student variables. They get grades in school, probably some good, some bad, some indifferent. They are, or are not, as the case may be, "satisfied," either by school, or by their grades, or by both, in various degrees. They "perceive," or not, maybe, something called "teacher-directiveness." How can these things be seen as functions of one another?

Before we can begin this research, we have to be clear about some things that might confuse mere laymen. Notice first that whether a teacher actually *is* "directive" or not is not at issue; all that matters is whether a student "perceives" a teacher as "directive." This is child-centered research. Although grades do go into the hopper, it's not because we are interested in what a student has learned or how that can be measured, but because we want to know about the student's "satisfaction," which depends only in part on his grade, which must be factored in with his own perception of directiveness and his own student variables. This is still child-centered research.

Bearing in mind those warnings, we can now proceed with our research. If we are successful, we can expect to be able to answer questions like this:

Who will be more satisfied with a B plus, a moderately intelligent student with better than average convergent-divergent ability but little if any locus of control, or a very bright, dogmatic student who shows normal achievement orientation but no compulsivity to speak of and does not, unlike the first student, perceive the teacher as directive?

You can devise other such examples for yourself. The possibilities are probably infinite. None of them, however, will have any objective meaning, which would require a precise numerical evaluation of hosts of human traits, beliefs, attitudes, prejudices, and emotions. In fact, that kind of study must end exactly where it begins, in a vague generalization. You and I, if asked and forced to answer, could also have said that there *may* be a *fair* degree of *moderate* intercorrelation between a person's characteristic traits and the way he feels about things. This is the kind of revelation that educationistic research provides.

It does that useless work, obviously more for profit than for fun, since it is impossible that even the dullest educationist can find the ecstasy of discovery in such an enterprise, precisely because it *is* child-centered. Here in the shadow of Wundt, education and the presumable content of an education are not the objects of the educationist's concern. It is the children, the students, who are to be studied, for the education is something that is being done to them with certain modifications in mind. While the originally intended modification may be nothing more than changing children who can't add into children who can, the process of modification itself is obviously more likely to produce a "scholarship" of the kind just cited than a mere counting of those who can add and those who can't. That scholarship, you surely noticed, is *not* about what children may have learned and how, but about how they feel; and it isn't even about how they feel about what they may have learned, but about how they feel about their *grades* and their *teacher*. If we could hope to learn anything from such research, it would be not about education but about children. But, following Wundt, that is exactly what we need to know, for "education" is the psychologically appropriate manipulation of learners. If that is so, the more we know about the manipulee the better.

That view of "education" is not entirely without merit. Some things can be taught to some people just that way, although the system works far more dependably with horses and dogs. But human beings are immensely different from one another even while they are very much alike, and even the most avidly child-centered educationists have not yet suggested an educational system in which every child, after a stupefying battery of psychological tests, is assigned a perfectly matched teacher, who has also had all those tests. Therefore, the teaching of anything has to be a compromise, a generalized set of stimuli aimed at producing the desired responses in *most* of the children. In some cases, therefore, it is bound to fail.

Several things can happen when education fails, none of them good. No. I will be more precise. None of them *can* be good as long as we think of education as the design of appropriate stimuli to produce certain behavior in an individual human being. If we do think that, then there are three things we can think of doing when some students fail to learn, since there are three factors in our equation — the stimulus, the student, the response.

We can change the stimulus. This is a big job, for it requires changing an already institutionalized compromise designed to elicit the right response from as many children as possible, a massive system. Nevertheless, it has been done. Every simplified revision of some already simplified text is just such a change, and so is the widespread use of films and even television programs in place of books. When such a change is made, of course, it is made in the supposed interests of those who have failed to respond appropriately. That accounts for the fact that methods of instruction are designed to accommodate not the most ordinary children, but those who learn most slowly.

We can also change the expected response. If some children do not seem to learn history, we can decide to teach them civic pride and responsibility instead. This is especially attractive if we have already decided that civic pride and responsibility might well be the proper student outcomes of the study of history anyway. This is a common device, of which I will have more to say in the next chapter.

We can even *try* to change the student. This is hardest of all, but educationists never give up. On this matter, too, there is much to say later, but for now we must look at what happens in the Wundtian system before or unless such a change can be made. What follows, along with some notably ghastly language, is a display of one of the educationist's most cherished devices, the psychological manipulator's last resort:

Nobody Here But Us Professionals

The works of Weischadle, associate professor of education at Montclair State College in New Jersey, can be studied at length in the New Jersey section of *The New York Times* for July 16, 1978. His piece is called, naturally, "Educating the Parents." Mass illiteracy he easily dismisses as a matter of "problem youngsters," but those uppity parents who are beginning to complain about illiteracy — they need to be taught a lesson. They can vote! If we don't straighten those malcontents out right away, they might end up listening to demagogues and voting against some of our favorite monies. Worse yet, and it's with this fear that Weischadle begins his finger-wagging, some of them might *win* those malpractice suits that they're discussing with their lawyers.

Weischadle protests that even if illiteracy *were* the fault of the schools, that wouldn't mean that the schools were to blame. Here's the delicate way he puts it:

> Have the critics been fair to the schools? To the extent that schools are responsible for a youngster's educational growth, the critics have dealt with the right party. However, it does not necessarily mean that professionals in the schools are inept. It does mean that educational leadership has failed to articulate the problem effectively and carry out the necessary programs.

It's hard to know exactly what Weischadle means by that "articulate." First we thought that the "professionals" had been unable to utter intelligible sounds, for that reading does reflect experience. However, in this kind of writing, no "professional" would ever waste a nifty word like "articulate" on such a simple thought. Next we guessed that the man might be saying that the "professionals" had been unable to define the problem thoroughly and accurately. That, too, we had to reject. Such inability would be remarkably similar to ineptitude in "professionals," surely, but Weischadle says they're *not* inept. Only one possibility remains: "To articulate the problem effectively" must mean to find some description that will keep irate parents from thinking that the "professionals" are inept. Of course! That's just what Weischadle is up to in this piece — *educating* the parents.

He does some pretty fancy articulating as well. Where do they learn that language? In the ordinary graduate school, candidates are expected to be competent in a couple of foreign languages, but in those education places they know that skill in language will cripple the budding "professional" by enabling him to say things plainly. You get no monies that way. Straight talk would mean the end of effective articulation as we know it.

Here are some examples of bent talk from Weischadle's little piece. He won't say that people are talking about something; he says that "much recent discussion has focused on" it. He can't say, "Hurry"; he says that "delay should not be allowed to take place." He can't say that people should use wisely what they have; he says that "an enlightened utilization . . . must be present." He can't say that the people who deal out discipline should be consistent; he says that "the haphazard application of disciplinary action . . . must be eliminated." He can't say, "Don't worry." He says that "uneasiness should be settled."

Still, we worry. For one thing, there is no clear meaning in the settling of uneasiness. In fact, it sounds ominous. If the settling of uneasiness has the same effect as the settling of terms or plans, we don't want any part of it. For another, how can we take any comfort from a teacher of teachers who condescends, in broken English, to explain why we should have "complete confidence" in him and other "professionals," so that they may get on, unhampered by our ill-informed and amateurish complaints, with the "acquisition . . . of monies to enact better programs" that will, *this* time around, solve the illiteracy problem?

In these examples of Weischadle's tortured English, the grammatical subjects are things, not persons, and abstract things at that. All things that must be done by people, but we see no people. This language suggests a world where responsible agents, the doers of deeds, have been magically occulted by the deeds themselves. A weird structure of that sort, "utilization must be present," for example, has the merit (?) of excusing somebody from an obligation to use something. If things go wrong, therefore, it's not any *person's* fault; it's just that utilization wasn't present.

Such structures, furthermore, often generate certain morally flavored auxiliary verbs: "delay should not" — "application must," etc. This is another grammatically symbolized cop-out which implies that moral obligation falls upon deeds rather than doers. It is up to those negligent deeds to get themselves done. This is convenient for those "professionals" who won't be able to do them.

Normal English, in its typical structure, a simple sentence in the active voice, implies a world where agents perform acts. There are times when we would wish it otherwise, and in our minds we can devise subterfuges that will make it seem otherwise. We do the business of the mind in language, and we make our subterfuges of the same stuff. Weischadle, in his grammatical gyrations, is not just writing bad English; he is positing a certain kind of world. In that world, one can *parler sans parler* like Castorp and reject in advance all responsibility for what one says. Here's how Weischadle does it — indeed, how almost anyone of those "professionals" would do it: "The pre-school years have been recognized as being important formulative years."

He probably means "formative," although he may be thinking that the pre-school years are the years spent sucking a formula from bottles — but no matter. The important thing is the grotesque contortion by which he escapes having to say that the pre-school years *are* formative, or, if you like, formulative. It matters not at all to the "professional" that what he has to say is obvious and banal and widely enough known that it needs no saying; he still finds a way to evade responsibility for having said it. In this timid language of misdirection and abdication, no one would dare stand forth and proclaim that a turkey is a turkey. He might mutter, tentatively, that a turkey has been recognized as being a turkey — although not necessarily by *him*.

Into such prose, human beings vanish. No wonder we couldn't discover Weischadle's salary. He has withdrawn into the precincts of the passive voice. He has given over all doing of deeds and drawn up about him the mists of circumlocution. Far from our ken, he has sojourned in the land of the self-eliminating application and followed the spoor of the place-taking delay. He is, by now, by gloomy night and periphrastics compassed round. He is, in short, or sort of short, no longer recognized as being Weischadle. Now we see the truth. There *is* no Weischadle.

❖ ── ❖

What could be more obvious? When the object of a psychological manipulation fails to respond in the usual way, there must be something wrong with him. This conclusion is the same as the neurologist's, for whom the failure of a knee to jerk has one ominous significance. In Wundt's psychology, the mind itself is held to be, *must* be if the system is to be concretely scientific, a neurological phenomenon, and a predisposition against arithmetic must be a psycho-neurological aberration. Thus we must conclude, when children fail to respond appropriately to tested stimuli, that they have learning problems. That being so, it becomes the aim of educational research to find out all about learning problems and to discover, naturally, that the schools are full of "problem youngsters" harboring hosts of hitherto un-suspected "learning disabilities." From this preoccupation with pathology, the teacher-training profession takes many benefits.

One of them, of course, is simply the opportunity to do what can pass for scholarship or research, which leads to promotion and pay and to government grants. There would be little hope of such things in a simpler calling like plumbing. Plumbers install plumbing, and, when something goes wrong with the plumbing, they fix it. They don't care how the pipes feel about it. Teaching reading and arithmetic is much more like plumbing than you probably think. If you know how to read and cipher, you can, if you want to, teach those skills to almost any child in America. The chances are, too, that you will do a better job of it, and in a shorter time, than the schools. If you know *a lot* about mathematics and have paid thoughtful attention to language, you can do a *much* better job, and better by far, probably, than anything you can manage with your plumbing. But if the teaching of children were handled that way, simply by people who knew the skills and knowledge they were teaching, and who wanted simply to teach them, then a vast and comfortable empire would fall.

That empire is not, however, the empire of the schools. It is the empire of the teacher-training establishment. Most of what is taught and studied in the teacher academy has nothing to do with the subject matter that the teacher-trainees will someday teach. Teacher-training is itself "child-centered," and the teacher-trainees are themselves among the children. That's why so many education courses are devoted either to "enhanced self-awareness" or to a clinical scrutiny of children as psychological entities. The training of teachers is thus a miniature lampoon of the training of the psychoanalyst, who must first be analyzed so that he may do unto others as has been done unto him. The incipient teachers are to be, in fact, therapists, keen to discover, if unable to treat, vast arrays of "learning disabilities" and "problem youngsters." Teacher-training, therefore, is a colossal and terribly serious enterprise. It calls for more and more courses and workshops and "hands-on" laboratory "experiences" and in- and pre-service training, all of which require larger and larger faculties and counselors and facilitators and support services and more and more money. Without Wundt, none of this would be possible, and the teaching of children would be degraded into nothing more than an honest, honorable, skilled trade.

Wundt may have been wrong, but he was honest. He just wanted to know what he thought could be known. His bequest to us, marvelously transformed, is essentially a metaphor, an ideal paradigm of the process of education. We seem to imagine that there is something "wrong" with children, and that we must fix it. But by that "wrongness" we don't mean something simple to fix, like the perfectly normal ignorance of arithmetic in one who has not been taught arithmetic. We mean something more like a perverse bias against arithmetic, an innate predisposition whose remedy lies in some "treatment" or other. We can see that the treatment, therefore, must take priority, for the arithmetic depends on the treatment, the modification of behavior. Thus we will first make the student whole, through devising and applying appropriate stimuli, so that he can, if it still seems desirable, learn his arithmetic. This paradigm does not include the proposition, certainly questionable but just as certainly intriguing, that we can make the student whole by *teaching* the arithmetic.

The Seven
Deadly Principles

After sober and judicious consideration, and weighing one thing against another in the interests of reasonable compromise, H. L. Mencken concluded that a startling and dramatic improvement in American education required only that we hang all the professors and burn down the schools. His uncharacteristically moderate proposal was not adopted. Those who actually knew more about education than Mencken did could see that his plan was nothing more than cosmetic and would in fact provide only an outward appearance of improvement. Those who knew less, on the other hand, had somewhat more elaborate plans of their own, and they just happened to be in charge of the schools.

Those who knew less, to be specific, were the members of the National Education Association's Commission on the Reorganization of Secondary Education, a.k.a. The Gang of Twenty-seven, now long forgotten but certainly not gone. They builded better than they knew, and their souls go marching on in every school in America today. The Commission was established in 1913, the year that also brought us the income tax. Many of its members were functionaries of school bureaucracies, from the United States Commissioner of Education himself down through supervisors and associate superintendents and principals and even a high school inspector, whatever that was, to no less a personage than a senior educational secretary of the YMCA. Professors and assistant professors of education represented the higher learning. One of *them* was chairman of the committee on mathematics, naturally, while the committees on lesser disciplines, notably classical and modern languages, were directed by high school teachers. The stern sciences were served by a professor of education, while the smiling sciences like social studies and the other household arts were overseen by federal bureaucrats. In the whole motley crew there were no scientists, no mathematicians, no historians, no traditional scholars of any sort.

That was surely no accident, for it seems to have been an article of the Commission's unspoken agenda to overturn the work of an earlier NEA task force that *had* been made up largely of scholars, the Committee of Ten, called together in 1892 and chaired by Charles W. Eliot, then president of Harvard University. That committee had come out in favor of traditional academic study in the public schools, which they fancied should be devoted to the pursuit of knowledge and the training of the intellect. But what can you expect from a bunch of intellectuals? The Eliot Report of 1893 was given to things like this:

> As studies in language and in the natural sciences are best adapted to cultivate the habits of observation; as mathematics are the traditional training of the reasoning faculties; so history and its allied branches are better adapted than any other studies to promote the invaluable mental power which we call judgment.

Obviously, the Eliot committee did its work in the lost, dark days before the world of education had discovered the power of the bold innovative thrust. All they asked of the high schools was the pursuit of knowledge and the exercise of the mind in the cause of judgment.

The Gang of Twenty-seven, unhampered by intellectual predispositions, found that proposal an elitist's dream. They concluded, in other words, that precious few schoolchildren were capable of the pursuit of knowledge and the exercise of the mind in the cause of judgment. That, of course, turned out to be the most momentous self-fulfilling prophecy of our century. It is also a splendid example of the muddled thought out of which established educational practice derives its theories. The proposals of the Eliot report are deemed elitist because they presume that most schoolchildren are generally capable of the mastery of subject matter and intellectual skill; the proposals of the Commission on the Reorganization of Secondary Education, on the other hand, are "democratic" in presuming that most schoolchildren are *not* capable of such things and should stick to homemaking and the manual arts.

This bizarre principle is still very much with us as a generator of educationistic theory and practice. It shows, among other things, the immense power of words, especially nasty ones like "elitism," notably abhorrent to our egalitarian society. It is certainly true (and puzzling as well, since the men who made us this egalitarian society were indubitable intellectuals) that we distrust intellectuals. They *do* seem to be an elite, although, thank goodness, a powerless elite. They butter little bread. Nevertheless, when we ask those intellectuals what we should do in the schools, they tell us to do everything we can to bring forth swarms of other intellectuals, which must lead us to conclude that the intellectual elitists can't be too smart. What kind of an elitist can it be who wants to generate his own competitors, and lots of them at that? But the champions of a "democratic" public education, righteous enemies of elitism, rejoice in the profitable belief that hardly any of the children in their charge can expect to rise to the level of curriculum facilitator, to say nothing of superintendent of schools.

In the cause of "democratic" public education, the Gang of Twenty-seven compounded illogic with ignorance by deciding that the education proposed by the Eliot committee was primarily meant as "preparation for the college or university." True, relatively few high school graduates of 1913 went on to college; but even fewer had done so in 1893. Indeed, it was just *because* so few would go on to more education that the Eliot committee wanted so many to have so much in high school. But the Gang of Twenty-seven decided that since very few students would go on to the mastery of a discipline and the rigorous training of the mind in college, which colleges were still fancied to provide in those days, there was little need to fuss about such things in high school. They had far more interesting things to fuss about in any case, *their* kinds of things. They enshrined them all, where they abide as holy relics of the cult of educationism to this day, in their final report, issued in 1918 (and printed at government expense, like all the outpourings of educationism ever since) as *Cardinal Principles of Secondary Education.*

Cardinal Principles was a small pamphlet, not much larger than *The Communist Manifesto* or a man's hand. It rejected the elitist and undemocratic education of the dark past and provided in its place "preparation for effective living." It made us the effective livers we are today, and it sends forth every year from our public schools and colleges all those effective livers who will make the future of the nation.

The seven cardinal principles were put forth as the paths to the seven "main objectives of education," which had finally been discovered once and for all after twenty-five hundred years of intellectual floundering. The first of those main objectives was *Health*. *Health*. Its primacy is justified by that firm grasp on the obvious that was to become the very foundation stone of educational theorizing: "Health needs cannot be neglected during the period of secondary education without serious danger to the individual and the race." How true. You can't make effective livers out of dead children. And think of the race! Suppose they *all* die! How then will we get the taxpayers "to secure teachers competent to ascertain and meet the needs of individual pupils and able to inculcate in the entire student body a love for clean sport?"

(It is interesting to notice that, like this one, all of the proposals in *Cardinal Principles* will call for vastly increased faculties and administrative bureaucracies both in the high schools and in the teachers' colleges. This has since become the Eighth Cardinal Principle, which you can see doing its work in your local school system whenever any remedy to any problem or shortcoming is proposed: Whatever we do will require more money, more teachers, more administrators, and more mandated courses in education.)

Cardinal Principles even proposed that there be in each school a kind of health officer, whose job would range from looking around for insanitary conditions in the building to inquiring into the social lives of the students, who might well be risking their health in the streets and in ice-cream parlors. It was in the cause of health, I believe, that my own first-grade teacher used to hold fingernail inspection every morning and cry out now and then to some slouching young reprobate: "Posture!" It was in this cause, too, that what was called "physical education" became the oppressive monster that it is today and, by the very power of its name, compounded beyond remedy the educationistic delusion that "education" and "training" are the same thing. It is not a coincidence, nor is it without large consequences, that so many of America's high school principals were once phys. ed. teachers.

The second "main objective" is, at first, slightly surprising: *Command of Fundamental Processes*. In 1918 that meant just about what Basic Minimum Competence means today. Although it certainly did not mean anything *more* than Basic Minimum Competence either, it did at least mean a higher minimum. Nowadays we count ourselves lucky if the students can read and write at the ninth-grade level, whatever that means this year. *Cardinal Principles* says that such a level of competence, even in 1918, "is not sufficient for the needs of modern life." (I must say, too, that *Cardinal Principles*, although stilted and dull, is not written in the self-serving, mindless jargon of today's educationists. This credit, however, must be balanced against a large debit. It was in the ensuing scramble of silly, pseudo-scholarship required for the justification of the cardinal principles that our educationists discovered the power of mendacious gobbledegook and adopted it as their native tongue.)

Furthermore, it is clear that, while the drafters of *Cardinal Principles* do put Command of Fundamental Processes second only to Health, they do so apparently as an involuntary bend of the knee to that discredited old elitism. About the other "main objectives" they have a lot to say, and many suggestions as to how curriculum might be manipulated in their accommodation and many new people hired in their cause. When they have called for Command of Fundamental Processes, that's it. They proceed at once to *Worthy Home-membership*, a main objective much more to their liking.

Cardinal Principles admits, affirms, in fact, that "In the education of every high-school girl, the household arts should have a prominent place because of their importance to the girl herself and to others whose welfare will be directly in her keeping." It presumes, too, that even girls who do idle away a few more years in college or in "occupations not related to the household arts" will someday have to face their "actual needs and future responsibilities" and "understand the essentials of food values, of sanitation, and of household budgets."

Although Worthy Home-membership obviously has a lot to do with cooking and sewing, it also provides for the dilution of whatever may persist of the old elitist curriculum:

> The social studies should deal with the home as a fundamental social institution and clarify its relation to the wider interests outside. [That will disqualify history, a discipline notably unconcerned with "the home," as a worthy study.] Literature should interpret and idealize the human elements that go to make the home. [That knocks out the study of literature, which is remarkably unlikely to do what some educationists decree that it "should" do.] Music and art should result in more beautiful homes and greater joy therein. [They really had to stretch for that one, but it will call to order pretentious art and music teachers who peddle their subjects as

intrinsically worthwhile, and it will even justify the in-
clusion of interior decorating in the high school curriculum.]

It is exactly that, the dilution of ordinary academic study,
that makes this kind of "education" so pernicious. Obviously
no one can object to housekeeping skills or to beautiful
homes and joy therein. But beauty and joy, and even housekeeping skills, are either diminished or destroyed by ignorance and stupidity, which are likely to flourish in a
place where history is subordinated to a "social study" of the
home as an institution and where literature is chosen for
study if it does what it "should" do.

Those funny "educations" are all the more powerful and
long-lived because they are designed to grow fat and sassy
through eating the bodies of their victims. When we embark
on an ambitious program of Worthy Home-membership
Education, we justify ourselves by naming some indubitable
benefits we intend to bestow: an understanding of "the essentials of food values, of sanitation, and of household
budgets," for instance. Those benefits, of course, can be had,
along with a great deal more, by those who study and learn
such things as biology, chemistry, and mathematics, but
those stern old disciplines offer little scope for the bold, innovative thrust and the increased budget. So we pretend, or
some of us may actually believe, that home budgeting, which
is a skill all these girls need, can be learned in the *absence*
of mathematics, which is an elitist skill useful only for a few.

And sure enough — little by little the study and practice
of such subjects as science and mathematics decline, and
fewer and fewer students take such courses. We have helped
this decline by providing easy and "democratic" options for

those who seem to have a little trouble with the demanding elitism of traditional academic study. Now the day has come when very few high school girls can do any arithmetic at all. Now is our triumph. We can redignify Worthy Home-membership Education with a trendy new name, Consumer Education, and teach nutrition and wary shopping to girls who are innocent of science and unable to figure out the price of an ounce of macaroni. Those deficits, which flow from our very existence, we can now put forth as arguments for our continued existence. This pattern, of course, can describe the growth and triumph of any of those "educations."

Another such education was the fourth main objective in *Cardinal Principles*: *Vocation*. The Commission's proposals for a vocational education program that would take up "much of the pupil's time" derive from its own cardinal principles: that few students can do academic work and would best spend their time in learning homemaking skills and trades, and that the larger purpose of public education was to bring about a certain social order. They urge vocational education not only to "equip the individual to secure a livelihood for himself and those dependent on him," but also so that he may "maintain the right relationships toward his fellow workers and society." The Commission does not, of course, explain what "right relationships" might be, perhaps presuming that all the other educationists who read their report would surely favor right relationships over wrong relationships without giving the matter any thought. As usual.

But vocational education, as imagined in *Cardinal Principles*, was not to be a separate program within the schools; it was intended that even those students who did not spend "much of their time" in the wood shop would nevertheless "develop an appreciation of the significance" of vocations "and a clear conception of right relations [there they are again] between the members of the chosen vocation, between different vocational groups, between employer and employee, and between producer and consumer." All such things can be studied, of course, in the context of several well-known disciplines, but study can provide only knowledge. *Cardinal Principles* does not call for *knowledge* of these matters, however, but for "appreciation" and a "clear conception of right relations."

It is a thematic illusion of our educational enterprise that understanding can be had without knowledge, that the discretion can be informed without information, that judgment need not wait on evidence. Before we can ask what *are* the right relations between producer and consumer, for instance, we must know what are all the *possible* relations between producer and consumer. We must know antecedents and consequences; we must know functions and contexts. We must, in fact, know more than we can hope to know, which is why thoughtful people only reluctantly and armed with as much knowledge as possible leap from knowing into judging and decide to "hold" some truths self-evident.

On the other hand, *Cardinal Principles*, in speaking of its fifth main objective, *Civics Education*, leaps blithely into: "Too frequently, however, does mere information, conventional in value and remote in its bearing, make up the content of the social studies." Mere information. What the Commission might mean by "conventional in value" I just don't know, but I do know, along with all who have ever studied, that only a fool is willing to take the risk that this or that bit of mere information is "remote in its bearing." Facts seem unrelated only to those who know few facts.

As you might expect, Civics Education — what a noble cause! — is given enormous power to alter and dilute the content of traditional academic subjects:

> History should so treat the growth of institutions that their present value may be appreciated. Geography should show the interdependence of men while it shows their common dependence on nature. Civics should concern itself less with constitutional questions and remote governmental functions, and should direct attention to social agencies close at hand and to the informal activities of daily life that regard and seek the common good. Such agencies as child-welfare organizations and consumers' leagues afford specific opportunities for the expression of civic qualities by the older pupils.
>
> The work in English should kindle social ideals and give insight into social conditions and into personal character as related to these conditions. Hence the emphasis by the committee on English on the importance of a knowledge of social activities, social movements, and social needs on the part of the teacher of English.

And, not content with prescribing an "appreciation" of institutions that would satisfy Lenin, ignorance of the constitution in the name of responsible citizenship, and literature as an instigator of social compliance, the Commission decides also that "*all* subjects should contribute to good citizenship." (My italics.) While they would probably not suggest, in that cause, that the binomial theorem be put to a vote in class, their descendants and adherents *will*, in fact, suggest that mathematics, obviously "remote in its bearing" on good citizenship, is not really at the heart of the educational enterprise.

While its concrete proposals for Civics Education are very

much like its proposals for all the other educations, *Cardinal Principles*, in the name of "attitudes and habits important in a democracy," goes an extra step and prescribes what should actually happen in the classroom. It urges "the assignment of projects and problems to groups of pupils for cooperative solution and the socialized recitation whereby the class as a whole develops a sense of collective responsibility. Both of these devices give training in collective thinking." Here we can see the theoretical foundations of the rap session, the encounter group, the values clarification module, and the typical course in education, but also something far worse.

For thousands of years, many decent, knowing, and thoughtful people have hated and feared democracy, and with good reasons. We don't think of it that way any longer, probably because we have all been to schools devoted to the cardinal principles, but the framers of our society took great pains to guard us against the obvious (to them) dangers inherent in majority rule. It was precisely to commend and elucidate the constitution's ability to protect the few from the ignorance or self-interest of the many that Madison wrote the tenth Federalist Paper, which is, of course, not included in the Civics Education curriculum. The children who are to generate "cooperative solutions" and "socialized recitations" are to do so without concern for, or even any knowledge of, "constitutional questions and remote governmental functions" like checks and balances. They will do their "collective thinking" unencumbered by "mere information."

It is another of the educationists' self-serving delusions that if enough of the ignorant pool their resources, knowledge will appear, and that a parliament of fools can deliberate its way to wisdom. This delusion is not entirely groundless. It is grounded in another delusion, the one that flows from a half-baked adaptation of the work of Wundt.

You will recall Cattell's curious conclusion that learning the sounds of letters was not useful in learning to read because those who could read did not sound out the letters. Recall also that Wundt saw *learning* (he did *not* say "education") as a conditioned response to stimuli. For American educationists, such "facts" were absorbed into a generalized notion that might be put something like this: We notice that educated people, whatever that might mean, have certain attributes and that they do things in certain ways, or, since we are educationists, that they "exhibit certain behaviors." So, if our students come to have those attributes and exhibit those behaviors, they will be educated, and we will be educators.

Educated and thoughtful people have indeed often met and deliberated together and solved problems and found wisdom. Just look at the Constitutional Convention, for example, or, if you're a little short on mere information, consider the Commission on the Reorganization of Secondary Education. Therefore, if we assign projects and problems to groups of students we will instill in them the same "sense of collective responsibility" that we see so often among the educated and thoughtful. In that fashion, furthermore, we will engender in them an appropriate appreciation of "the ideals of American democracy and loyalty to them," as *Cardinal Principles* recommends.

An analogous line of reasoning would begin with the observation that musicians have been known to play "Lady of Spain" and end with the determination to train seals to play "Lady of Spain" on bicycle horns and turn them into musicians.

And there is another ominous and far-reaching implication in the Commission's assignment of projects and problems hidden, not very deeply, in "collective thinking." This phrase reveals an appalling ignorance and thoughtlessness out of which terrifying educationistic malfeasances have been growing for decades.

Schooling is done in public places, but the roots of an education can grow only in the hidden ground of the mind. Lessons are taught in social institutions, but they can be learned only by private people. The acts that are at once the means and the ends of education, knowing, thinking, understanding, judging, are all committed in solitude. It is only in *a* mind that the work of the mind can be done. There is no such thing as "collective thinking." Our schools can be an instrument for socialization or an incentive to thoughtfulness, but they cannot be both.

Thus it is, for instance, that such elementary skills as reading and writing, public analogues of private thinking, are so ill taught in the schools. It is not sufficient explanation of this failure to point out that the educationists who design the schools are themselves notoriously poor readers and writers, although they are. That leads us only to ask in turn why *that* should be so. At the root of our widespread and institutionalized illiteracy is a fevered commitment to socialization and an equally unhealthy hostility to the solitary, and thus probably antisocial, work of the mind. In school, the inane and uninformed regurgitations of the ninth-grade rap session on solar energy as a viable alternative to nuclear power are positive, creative, self-esteem–enhancing student behavioral outcomes; the child who sits alone at the turning of the staircase, reading, is a weirdo. The students did not bring that "appreciation" to school; they learned it there.

Somewhat later in their history, the educationists will justify and formalize their hostility to the intellect, with which they never *did* feel comfortable, by inventing the "affective domain" of feelings and attitudes and appreciations and setting its gracious virtues over against the tedious and unimaginative "rote" learning of the merely "cognitive domain." But they will only raise walls where the Gang of Twenty-seven has dug the foundation. We can see the marks of their shovels in all those appreciations and attitudes and values and "worthy" attributes of this and that. And when they come to their sixth main objective of secondary education, *Worthy Use of Leisure*, they outdo their successors in a sublime presumptuousness possible only to the happily and profoundly ignorant.

As to the Worthy Use of Leisure, they counsel thus:

> Heretofore the high school has given little conscious attention to this objective. It has so exclusively sought intellectual discipline that it has seldom treated literature, art, and music so as to evoke right emotional response and produce positive enjoyment. Its presentations of science should aim, in part, to arouse a genuine appreciation of nature.

So. Intellectual discipline is not compatible with "right emotional response" and "positive enjoyment." And a pack of manual arts teachers, educationists, and bureaucrats can tell us what a right emotional response would be, presumably. They can clarify for us, without any tedious attention to inorganic chemistry or the laws of motion, not only an appreciation of nature but a *genuine* appreciation of nature. They are bestowers of blessings on the benighted. Their discoveries, however, would probably come as a sad surprise to Jefferson, who, in spite of his command of intellectual disciplines, labored all his life under the delusion that he *did* take "positive enjoyment" from literature, art, and especially from music.

One of the characteristics of the mind of educationism, just as much now as in the days of *Cardinal Principles*, is an apparent inability to follow paths of thought far enough to discover contradictions in logic. If scientific research, or technological craftsmanship, for that matter, were as little given to self-examination as educationistic theory, we would have practically nothing that worked. The notion that intellectual discipline is somehow an impediment to "right response," a notion that we find not only in the context of the arts but everywhere in *Cardinal Principles* and in subsequent educationistic theorizing, must eventually lead us to the conclusion that those who hold it cannot be believed. It is, after all, by virtue of some fancied "intellectual discipline" in themselves that educationistic theorists claim to prescribe the "right" responses, attitudes, and appreciations that are precluded by intellectual discipline.

This is not only illogical but even antisocial, which is another disabling contradiction in a theory proposing schooling as a means of socialization. They say, in effect, that *students* who are needlessly led into intellectual discipline will not achieve right emotional response, but that educationists are *not* thus handicapped. It is a strange sort of teacher who says in his heart that his students need never know what he knows. That goes far beyond elitism; it is cultism. If a teacher is dedicated to knowledge and thought, he works in the hope that his students, some of them, one of them, will come to know and think more than he does, for only thus can knowledge and thought be served. To treat his students, or some of them, or even one of them, as though they could never know and think what he knows and thinks, suggests a dedication to something else. Perhaps to his job. Perhaps he fears to raise up what such a teacher would surely think of as competition. While an individual teacher, of course, need have no realistic fears that some student will supplant him, the same is not true of the ideologues who claim to define the whole system of teaching and learning. How convenient it is, we notice, for the future welfare of the commissioners that *they* are immune to the nasty side effects of intellectual discipline from which they will magnanimously shelter the children.

I must note, at this point, that the Commission on the Reorganization of Secondary Education was assembled by the National Education Association, a widely misunderstood outfit. The ordinary citizen reads its pronouncements in the newspapers from time to time and notices that it gives its seal of approval to treacly television shows and elementary dramatizations of popular "classics." He has the impression that the NEA is something "official." But it is, of course, as it was in 1918 and long before, a trade union. That it should be called on to set national policy in the public schools is like putting the teamsters' union in charge of traffic laws and the licensing of drivers, but even more so. We have accepted the determinations of a teachers' union as to how America should be educated only because the job of designing an educational system is so hideously boring that only those whose self-interest is clearly at stake will undertake it. Our corporate self-interest, to be sure, is also very much at stake, but not *clearly*, at least not clearly enough for the ordinary citizen, who cannot see beyond the fact that all questions of education and schooling are hideously boring.

The self-interest of a massive educationists' trade union is evident on every page of *Cardinal Principles*. Whether that self-interest influences the document in partnership with shabby habits of thought, or whether those habits are themselves the consequences of the self-interest, who can say? But the result is the same. In every "main objective" we can find generous provision for the employment of growing hosts of dues-paying members of the NEA. It is also assured that much room will be made in the academic world for a new class, the arrivistes of educationism, the guidance counselors and curriculum facilitators, the physical education and typing teachers, the appreciation experts and the right emotional response imparters, the fingernail inspectors, and the right relationships inducers, who can launch themselves easily into secure and respectable careers without worrying about the burdensome demands of mere information and intellectual discipline.

In the world projected in *Cardinal Principles*, there is no place for scholars or scholarship. The whole, vast enterprise of training the minds that will shape the thought and knowledge of the future is dealt with in exactly one sentence: "Provisions should be made also for those having distinctly academic interests and needs." Exactly what provisions the Gang of Twenty-seven might have had in mind, we'll never know, although their provisions for the supervision of habits of hygiene and social events are detailed at length. We have to wonder, too, how such provisions could be made at all, given that "Each subject now taught in high school is in need of extensive reorganization in order that it may contribute more effectively to the objectives outlined herein, and the place of that subject in secondary education should depend on the value of such contribution." By that principle, any course of study that might attract those wretched misfits with academic interests, an intellectual discipline clogged with mere information, would have to be either diluted into the pursuit of appreciation or simply eliminated. That, of course, has happened.

(All is not lost, however. In any school there are a few teachers who didn't know what they were getting into when they went to the teachers' college and have stoutly — and usually silently — retained their devotion to intellectual discipline and even improved their stores of mere information in spite of having to give most of their time to education courses. They are the unintended "provision . . . for those having distinctly academic interests and needs." That's why every educated person you know will give special credit to this or that certain teacher. Such teachers, however, are seldom popular with their colleagues, and never with the administrators, so they often have to work underground. No matter. Those weird students will find those weird teachers and will learn from them, in any subject at all, something of the work of the mind.)

In fact, the Commission on the Reorganization of Secondary Education was simply not interested in students with "distinctly academic needs and interests." It began by assuming that there were few of those in any case, and ended by projecting an "education" that would make them even fewer. In the Commission's plan there was as little concern for academic talent as there was space on the page for naming the provisions, for the commissioners were, deep down where it really counted, not teachers at all but Sunday-school supervisors *manqués*, officious and ill-informed laymen busily hastening to good make-works and armed with the serene self-confidence that only ignorance can provide. They wanted to be not teachers but preachers, and prophets too, charging themselves with the cure of the soul of democracy and the raising up in the faith of true believers. They made concrete and formal the anti-intellectual dogmatism that characterizes our schools today.

The seventh and last of the Commission's main objectives of secondary education was nothing less than *Ethical Character*, which they pronounced "paramount" in a *democratic* society, as if Plato, Epictetus, Saint Augustine, Voltaire, Kant, Spinoza, and so on, for countless thinkers who lived under all sorts of governments, had somehow missed the point now perfectly clear to certain manual arts teachers and associate superintendents. They were as smugly confident of their ability to engender Ethical Character through "the wise selection of content and methods of instruction in all subjects of study" as they were of their ability to tell right emotional response from wrong. All it takes, after all, is what they are certain they have: wisdom.

I have more to say later on the vexatious question of the role of public education, all too accurately described in *Cardinal Principles* as "the one agency that may be controlled definitely and consciously," in the supposed formation of Ethical Character. For now, it is useful to point to the obvious fact that you will have a hard time finding a citizen who is opposed to the formation of ethical character. Or to worthy use of leisure time. Or to health, or any of the "main objectives" of secondary education as discovered in *Cardinal Principles*. Those objectives can be seen to constitute what is essentially a political platform eminently acceptable to all those who are in favor of good and against evil. Public acceptance of that platform was all the more certain because there was, after all, no opposing party.

And how could there be? In this case, opposition could hardly be the simple recommendation of contrary "main objectives." No one would vote for some educational splinter group calling for sickness and degeneracy. The opposition, if there were to be any, would require in its adherents a precise and thorough attention to detail, the pursuit of logical argument, the formulation of hypotheses as to consequences, an underlying theory as to the means and ends of education, and some considerable knowledge of the history of human thought. Such a constituency will never be large. There was such a constituency, of course, as there always is, made up of thoughtful and educated people of all kinds, some of them actually in schools. But the scholarly, academic wing of that small party was not asked to the table with the members of the Commission on the Reorganization of Secondary Education, who didn't want to hear any more of that "traditional training of the reasoning faculties" stuff in the report of the Eliot committee. And the other political dissidents, the ones you might call the civilians in the school war, had other and far more important things to do. Most of them had probably never heard of *Cardinal Principles*, and those who had would surely have found it of little interest. The theorists of American public education, actually feeble and helpless creatures, have evolved an amazing power to protect themselves against predators by emitting an unbearable cloud of dullness and boredom.

If there is such a thing as an intellectual and cultural elite in America, and there may well be a far larger one than even its detractors imagine, it is surely worthy of condemnation, for it is selfish and lazy. Jefferson and his friends indubitably thought of themselves as an elite, a natural aristocracy of talent. So thinking, they saw themselves not as privileged but as obliged by their gifts, obliged to serve the common good by the simple fact of their ability to do so. This attitude is not rampant among us. It is especially un-rampant in the academic community, where those who more or less secretly *do* think of themselves as an elite have trained themselves to imagine that the dull business of public educa-tion has nothing to do with their high endeavors.

The underlying attitudes and beliefs in *Cardinal Principles* have not been mitigated by the passage of time or the pres-sure of momentous events. Quite to the contrary, they have been regularly reaffirmed and reinvigorated, both in theory and practice. The devisers of the Seven Deadly Principles set out not to teach certain skills and knowledge to hosts of children but to change the nature of American society. They succeeded. They didn't, of course, *make* the vast mass of the people stupid and uninformed, for that happens in the course of nature without any need for deliberate effort, but they did arrange that fewer and fewer would reach escape velocity and rise out of the vast mass of the stupid and uninformed. As the consequences of the deadly principles become evident, sometimes one by one and sometimes in whole hosts of troubles, the descendants of the Gang of Twenty-seven point them out as justifications for even more of the same, more schemes to alter a society already suffering from all the earlier alterations.

The seven "main objectives of education" are still the main objectives of education, although one of them, Command of Fundamental Processes, was always somewhat less main than the others and remains so now that it has been renamed Basic Minimum Competence, in which term the important word is "minimum." And it is exactly toward the achieve-ment of those objectives, especially the greater six, that the training and indoctrination of schoolteachers is directed. Earnest attention to the seventh is just not possible in this scheme, for it would require precisely those things that *Cardinal Principles* finds inimical to "right" and "worthy" values: stringent intellectual discipline and great stores of mere information. The professors of education are not interested in those things, for their own training and indoctrination are no different from what they visit upon their students. After all, what else have they to bestow? And the professors of everything else just don't want to be bothered, and what they *do* have to bestow they save for a few favored students who will in turn become the professors of everything else who just don't want to be bothered. Mencken was right.

The
Principles March On

The educationism that now informs our schools and teacher academies is an amalgam of post-Wundtian misunderstanding and the Sunday-school do-goodism of *Cardinal Principles.* From the former it takes its characteristically therapeutic and manipulative methods and devices, and from the latter its pious pretentions as an agent of social harmony and guardian of the public virtue. In one way, therefore, it is pseudo-scientific, and in the other, pseudo-religious. It is the devotion to contradictory principles of dubious validity that generates the mental climate of educationism and leads to that special fatuousness so typical of American educational thought, a vexing blend of the illogical and the sentimental.

As recently as 1971, the National Education Association undertook a project called "Schools for the 70's and Beyond." The ensuing "main report," "written primarily [*sic*] by Warren T. Greenleaf and Gary A. Griffin," was published as a slim volume: *A Call to Action.* Although it was clearly written in the shadow of growing discontent about schools, it urged at least consideration of "the thesis that school *excellence* narrowly defined, not school *failure* narrowly defined, has given us most of the problems that divide our nation in 1970" — an entertaining proposition, and one that would surely confirm the assertion in *Cardinal Principles* that too much attention to intellectual discipline inhibits right understanding. And the "argument" put forth in support of that thesis is itself a dramatic example of worthy disregard for mere information:

> It was not illiterate, backward men who spiked our residential skylines with steel forests of television antennas, spoiled our rivers with the defecations of a hundred "growth" industries, fouled our air with the sooty contrails of a thousand jet planes taking off daily, or choked our cities with automobiles that cost as much to park as to buy. That work was accomplished by men whose schooling enabled them to develop transistors, no-deposit-no-return bottles, pressurized cabins, and a 36-months-to-pay economy.

You say you want to understand how a modern technological society works? Well, now you know. Men with schooling cunningly trick the multitudes into buying television antennas and driving expensive cars. Educated elitists force decent citizens to travel in airplanes and callously require them to dispose of bottles at their own expense. It isn't the "illiterate, backward men" who visit these horrors on us; untainted by "excellence narrowly defined," *they* can manage only rape, murder, arson, and an occasional gas-station stickup.

This amazingly stupid oversimplification is perfectly typical of educational theory. It is typical, too, in its confusion of "education" with the ability to design transistors and to pressurize cabins, which is precisely the sort of thing *Cardinal Principles* had in mind when it spoke of vocational training. Such a confusion is inevitable, however, when the pursuit of intellectual discipline is seen as hostile to right and worthy understanding. Even a fairly elementary technology, that of the electrician or plumber, for example, depends on certain disciplined habits of mind and a suitably large mass of information. The designing of transistors may be more complicated, but it is essentially the same *kind* of enterprise as plumbing. A distrust of intellectual discipline must eventually become a distrust of *any* disciplined habits of mind and any traditional store of "mere information." Logically, therefore, the writers of *A Call to Action* might also have indicted plumbers and electricians, the plumbers for having connected us to sewage systems and thence to the spoiling of rivers, and the electricians for making it easy to plug in the television sets for whose sake we have bought all those antennas.

Anti-intellectualism is like anti-Semitism, which only *begins* with the hating of Jews. From there it goes on to the ferreting out of hitherto-unsuspected manifestations of Jewishness, and anti-intellectualism goes on even to the denigration of technology, and thus of the very vocational training that schools offer as one of many antidotes to intellectualism. One could reasonably expect, therefore, that vocational training in the schools must become a halfhearted and half-baked enterprise, whose obvious purpose is not the teaching of even a relatively simple technology but the segregation of students for whom even "appreciation" seems too difficult. That, as it happens, is the case.

The writers of *A Call to Action* do not rest their case on the malefactors who brought us industrial waste and install- ment payments, outrageous impositions probably dating from neolithic elitism. They go on to say that "It was not ignorant men who designed a rifle bullet that could spin end over end to increase its flesh-tearing capacity." That, they remind us, was done by men with "schooling in the far reaches of physics." Well, maybe to an educationist a tumbling bullet, like the barb on a spear or the juice on an arrowhead, really *does* seem to come from the far reaches of physics. That would make sense.

They name also those devious "men sufficiently well edu- cated to cite precedents from 200 years of American law" as the ones "who juggled school boundaries . . . to keep black children separate from white." It was *not*, they assure us, "back-country bumpkins" who evilly studied law in order to "manipulate city ordinances." The back-country bumpkins left that sort of thing to the overeducated gentry and just went on about the business of beating and shooting and lynching.

It is fascinating, of course, to hear those who operate the schools argue that because there are people who can build aircraft for profit and cite law in their own cause we may conclude that the schools have actually provided too much "excellence." What is even more fascinating is that this be- wildering and ignorant line of reasoning should find, appar- ently, no detractors among the vast membership of the National Education Association, many thousands of whom must have read and taken comfort from *A Call to Action*.

When I still fancied that the mindless and illogical utter- ances so common in Academe were the results simply of haste or carelessness, and long before I began to study the educationists' self-justifications in works like *Cardinal Principles* and *A Call to Action*, the following ominously suggestive article appeared in *The Underground Grammarian*:

Prostrate
Trouble at NJEA

There is a kind of thoughtlessness that is not exactly stupidity. It is a failing seen in ordinarily intelligent people who, under the influence of self-interest, prefer to evade clarity of thought in precise language, giving themselves instead to recitation of the vague and comfortable. They write prostrate prose in which they let themselves be walked all over by verbal inaccuracies and the failures of logic that those inaccuracies always cause. Such prose is especially dangerous because it often sounds like common sense around the old pot-bellied stove. We will consider a case of cracker-barrel cant from the ruminations of one James P. Connerton.

Connerton is the new executive director of the New Jersey Education Association. All we know of him is what we read in the NJEA *Review* of January, 1979, to wit, that he has now returned to New Jersey after ten years spent in unspecified enterprises "in Minnesota, North Dakota, South Dakota, Iowa, Michigan, and other states." How *many* other states, deponent saith not, but he *doth* say: "His goals are our goals. Our aspirations are his aspirations. Our joy and our pain are his joy and pain." The pain probably has to do with moving expenses.

Deponent is Frank Totten, the president of NJEA. Here's more of what he writes:

> Together we are the NJEA. All of us have made us what
> we are today. What we will be in 10 or 20 years depends on
> our determination, our forsight, our hard work, and our
> togetherness.
>
> Jim Connerton is determined, farsighted, hardworking
> and one of us. As in the past, we'll do it together. We will
> determine our future and the future will be better because
> we have worked together.
>
> Welcome home Jim. We need you. The present and the
> future will be better for us because we'll work through
> them together.

That has a quaint charm, no? It sounds like the language in
which invocations are spoken at the firemen's annual clambake
and certificates of achievement awarded at Little League ban-
quets. Very American. However, we'd be readier to accept it —
even to applaud it — if only it had begun with the traditional
Unaccustomed As I Am. In this case, though, we might feel
more confident about the future of civilization if one of the
state's best-known schoolteachers seemed more accustomed to
written English, even to such trivia as comma splices and paragraph logic.

Never mind. Totten is only a harbinger. The har that he binges
is an article in which Connerton speaks *his* mind: "Our 'top'
priorities."

Strictly speaking, we can not name more than *one* priority, or
first thing, but the plural is irresistible to those who want to
dignify anything they think they may someday prepare to begin
to get ready to do something about or even just to think about.
When a word means almost anything, it means almost nothing.
To name something is to distinguish it from all the other things.

At the NJEA, they seem to have so many priorities that they
have to distinguish *them* from one another, calling *some* of them
"top" priorities. We must assume that they have also some middle
priorities and bottom priorities. Of top priorities, Connerton

explores a mere twelve. Here's what he says about a vexatious top priority indeed:

> Every reasonable person concedes that we can't hold the parent accountable for the color of a child's hair, that we can't rate the minister by the number of parishioners who break the Commandments, and that we can't blame the coach when a linebacker misses a tackle. Most people also concede that we can't judge teachers by the scores their students make on tests — especially on tests approved by some state office in Trenton that does not mesh with the local curriculum. Students should be evaluated by a variety of relevant measures, and so should teachers.

That "every reasonable person" is a rhetorical gimmick similar to a speaker's promise to make no mention of the well-known fact that his opponent is a thief and a pederast. In this case it is less effective, for it introduces either a shocking inanity or some hitherto unimagined cataclysm in genetics. But Connerton knows his audience. His pains are their pains, you'll recall, and they feel an almost intractable pain whenever they hear "accountable." By using the word in this context, he deludes readers into swallowing his absurdity, because they are predisposed to think that to hold parents "accountable" for attributes passed on to offspring is to castigate them for dereliction. If Connerton had said *that* in plain English, he would have avoided the absurd only to fall into the irrelevant. "Every reasonable person," and even some members of the NJEA, would have asked, So what else is new, Jim?

Having grounded his argument firmly on a proposition that is either preposterous or pointless, depending on how we understand "accountable," but having thereby won the hearts and minds of thoughtless readers, Connerton offers two further propositions meant to be analogous to the first. However, if they were plain statements of fact, which they are not, they could be analogous only to the irrelevant version of the first proposition. In order to be analogous to the *other* possible version, the absurd one, they would have to be obvious misrepresentations of fact, which they also are not. Therefore they are *not* analogous to the first proposition. In one way, that's lucky for Connerton, since even schoolteachers might be able to spot three logical monstrosities in a row. In another way, it's unlucky. His second and third propositions *are* analogous to the business of evaluating the effectiveness of teachers, and they suggest the opposite of what Connerton wants to say.

We can expect some normal amount of ox-coveting and idolatry in any congregation; but, should sinning increase inordinately and persist obstinately, as illiteracy has in the schools, we might indeed think to "rate" the shepherd of the flock. Furthermore, meek as they are, ministers would probably reject the implication that their work can be presumed to have no effect at all. Are teachers defending themselves by claiming that what *they* do cannot be presumed to have any effect? Why else would Connerton imply as much about the ministers? Maybe that's why we don't see those cute billboards anymore, the ones that used to say, "Teachers make the difference."

And those hard-eyed entrepreneurs who invest in football teams do indeed blame coaches — and fire them, too — when more and more linebackers miss more and more tackles. It's only amateurs who want to talk about "how you played the game." Does this analogy tell us that schooling should be judged as leniently as amateur athletics, and that we should be good sports, saying of each newly graduated illiterate, Well, that's how the ball bounces? If we were willing to concede that, do you suppose that Connerton would then concede that teachers should get the same salaries as those guys who coach the Little Leagues?

We have to presume, having heard of no mass defection from the NJEA, that most of the schoolteachers in New Jersey read this passage and found no fault in it. They were apparently content to find themselves defended in a ragged mishmash of non-sequiturs and false analogies that would earn a big fat F in any freshman logic course in the country. It must have reminded them of the papers that always guaranteed a big fat A, and perhaps even a cheerful, rubber-stamped smiling face, in all their education courses.

Whether or not Connerton knew what he was doing, who can say? But we *can* say that if he did he is an exceedingly clever writer, who knows that teachers are not too good at noticing fallacies. If he did *not* know what he was doing . . . well, that's not our problem. He is paid for the work of his mind not by taxpayers but by schoolteachers.

This tiny passage raises colossal questions: Does it reflect accurately the intelligent power of the average teacher in New Jersey? If so, we have given the teaching of our children into the care of the slow-witted. Or can it be that our teachers *can* see through this stuff but choose to let it stand because they *like* it, presuming (oh, so correctly) that it will prove effective in persuading a slow-witted public? Must we choose between dullness of mind and self-serving cynicism? What can we hope for where the interest of teachers is best served by the stupidity of the people? Do you *want* a world in which reasoning like Connerton's is accepted without question?

This is the most depressing text we have ever examined. It suggests a horrifying hypothesis, to wit, that, far from *failing* in its intended task, our educational system is in fact succeeding magnificently, because its aim is to keep the American people thoughtless enough to go on supporting the system. What educationists may *say* or even *believe* that they are doing is not to the point. Their self-interest is evident, and the cogency of their thinking is at least questionable. A hypothesis must be tested by reference to facts and its ability to account for the facts.

Now do your homework. Find some facts to test that dismal hypothesis. Brace yourself. You're going to have a bad day.

It may be only a coincidence that the passage cited is the work of a man who is in charge of an affiliate of the National Education Association, the people who brought us not only *Cardinal Principles* but our new Department of Education, but I don't think so. His pretense at argument is remarkably like that earlier bit about the wicked antenna-mongers. His audience is the same. His intention is the same: corporate self-justification. And, like the writers of *A Call to Action*, he can obviously write utter nonsense without any fear that his fellow educationists will expose him and call him to account. He is exercising the privileges of his membership in an extremely unusual sort of conspiracy, an unconscious conspiracy, if you can imagine such a thing, whose members are, in a very special sense, indubitably "innocent." They have no idea at all of what they are doing.

I want to repeat now a passage that appeared earlier and that may have seemed to you a trifle rash:

> We are people who imagine that we are weighing important issues when we exchange generalizations and well-known opinions. We decide how to vote or what to

buy according to whim or fancied self-interest, either of which is easily engendered in us by the manipulation of language, which we have neither the will nor the ability to analyze. We believe that we can reach conclusions without having the faintest idea of the difference between inferences and statements of fact, often without any suspicions that there are such things and that they *are* different. We are easily persuaded and repersuaded by what seems authoritative, without any notion of those attitudes and abilities that characterize authority. We do not notice elementary fallacies in logic; it doesn't even occur to us to look for them; few of us are even aware that such things exist. We make no regular distinctions between those kinds of things that can be known and objectively verified and those that can only be believed or not. Nor are we likely to examine, when we believe or not, the induced predispositions that may make us do the one or the other. We are easy prey.

Well, perhaps that sweeping "we" was rash, but the rest of it seems to me a fair description of people who can read about the antenna-mongers or Connerton's clergymen and coaches without dismay and fury. There is no evidence whatsoever that reasoning of that sort, which can be found wherever educationism is preached, arouses either fury or dismay or even a mild discontent. That fact, intriguing in itself, suggests some further facts about educationism, where the blind are led about by the one-eyed king.

It can lead us to take a closer look at educationistic "humanism," which, as you will remember, is the virtue for whose sake the educationists can hold that curious article of faith that finds intellectual achievement an inhibitor of effective teaching. In 1918 the Commission on the Reorganization of Secondary Education concluded, as we have seen, that the high schools had "so exclusively sought intellectual discipline" as to preclude "right emotional response." Although that inappropriate emphasis on intellectual discipline was soon replaced by hundreds of easy electives intended to ensure a satisfactory adjustment to life, the writers of *A Call to Action* discovered, in 1971, that there was still far too much of it. "We have," they say, speaking presumably for the NEA members who could read with gladness about those innocent back-country bumpkins, "overemphasized the intellectual development of students at the expense of other capacities." They called for less intellectual development and more attention to "other categories of human potential — emotional, social, aesthetic, spiritual, and physical — which suggest other directions for curricular reform."

There you have the beginnings of an understanding of the educationistic concept of "humanism." It has to do with those "other categories of human potential," other than intellectual, that is. This is a drastic transformation of a more well-known kind of humanism, in which it was quite specifically the human mind and its power of reason that gave the idea its name. Educationistic humanism is, in fact, so utterly unlike the system of thought ordinarily called by that name that I prefer to call the former by the name given it, although not *exclusively* in the cause of clarity, in the pages of *The Underground Grammarian*: "humanisticism." In humanism, it is the mind of man that is the type and discoverer at once of knowledge and understanding. In humanisticism, various feelings, or, as *Cardinal Principles* called them, "right emotional responses," seem to be thought of as the quintessential signs of being human. If we say of someone that he is a humanist, we suggest that he does the work of his mind in the expectation that he can devise knowledge and discover truth. The humanisticist, on the other hand, distrusts the work of the mind and seeks rather to *be* a certain kind of person than to *do* a certain kind of thing, expecting, it would seem, that knowledge and truth, relative things in any case, will become visible to the right kind of person.

The passage cited above, the one about the television antennas, is a splendid example of humanisticism, but certainly not of humanism. The humanist, too, would be repelled by filth and ugliness, but he would not find in it evidence of the inhumanity of the intellect in the "men whose schooling enabled them to develop transistors." On the contrary, he might lament the plight of the millions in whom the inadequately schooled intellect makes possible and profitable all those expensive automobiles and the forests of antennas. He would find in all our ugliness and filth a sad comment on the meagerness of mind out of which we so prize material comfort and convenience that we transform perfectly human and ingenious technological achievements into common nuisances. He would even be able to suggest a remedy in the form of a populace sufficiently skilled in the work of the mind so as to consider the probable consequences of materialistic appetite and thus make such public nuisances less profitable.

The humanisticist sees that ugliness and filth as the work of those in whom the work of the mind has engendered wrong feelings or, just as bad, an absence of feelings. In this he finds the baleful influence of "excellence narrowly defined," by which he seems to mean the development of intellectual, or at least, technical, skills without the simultaneous development of right feelings. He may also imply, but who can be sure, that intellectual discipline is hostile to the development of right feelings. That would seem to be the point in the later passage, where "other categories of human potential" are urged as an antidote to intellectual development. In effect, where the humanist says, If only we were thoughtful, the humanisticist says, If only we all felt the same way!

Humanisticism is sentimental, and in both senses of the word. The humanisticist sees the sentiments, or perhaps the human propensity to feel sentiments, as the quintessentially human attribute. He also puts faith, itself a sentiment, in what he considers either the evidence or even the conclusions of feelings, provided, of course, that they are "right" feelings. The delicious glow of sated greed, for instance, which might well have been the portion of those who *sold* all those antennas, although not of those who developed the theoretical understanding out of which they come, can *not* be trusted. It is not, in the language of *Cardinal Principles*, "worthy."

We can now reconsider a passage cited above, in which an educationistic "researcher" names "the personal characteristics related to transpersonal teaching":

(1) a view of man as essentially and inherently good at his core, (2) that the locus of power and authority in one's life is within the individual, and (3) that when dealing with life situations it is most effective to apply one's values to a solution with flexibility, and free of preconceptions or prejudice.

Those are surely decent sentiments, and they were almost certainly accepted and even applauded as such by the committee that granted the man who approved them a doctorate in education. They are also, of course, for what other kind can there be, "received" sentiments, often expressed, often approved, and sometimes even *felt*, at least in certain moods, by some human beings.

As a program for the practice of "transpersonal teaching," however, they may fail to satisfy. The goodness of man "at his core" needs some defining, and even some thought. Many will surely profess a belief that man is good at his core without having any idea what they mean by those terms and without any knowledge of the great history of human attempts to understand exactly what those terms might be taken to mean and whether such a belief could be justified by anything more than sentiment. Nevertheless, one who holds such a belief is free to hold it, of course, in a total absence of knowledge and thought. But what about one who not only holds that belief but even recommends it to others, or, as in this case, puts it forth as a belief that teachers should have if they want to be good, i.e., transpersonal? Or, to put it more practically, how can the teacher-trainers provide their students with "a view of man as essentially and inherently good at his core?"

Let's leave aside for now the question of *why* they should want to do that and ask only how it might be done. The intellectual study of the history of that belief will not suffice, for it is simply a fact that many who have pondered the proposition have concluded that it was either false or meaningless. In any case, the teacher-trainers are little likely to turn to intellectual study, which they already know to interdict right emotional response and to encourage the skepticism out of which men design transistors with no concern at all for the fact that transistors can be used in weapons. Where study will not serve, only precept and example remain. That's why the teachers of teachers, and then, of course, the teachers themselves, give much attention to the skill of "exhibiting behavior" of a certain kind. (That girl in the bunny outfit, whom you have probably forgotten, but I have not, was practicing just that — exhibiting a behavior calculated to arouse appropriate sentiments in little children.) If you behave like one who believes in man's good core, although exactly what deeds that might require I can't begin to imagine, then your students will come to believe, or at least come to believe that *you* believe. The behavior by itself, of course, will be ambiguous, perhaps even baffling, and unless you also tell your students what your behavior means they may well conclude that you're just a bit smarmy. Your acts and demeanor are "reinforcement" of the precept, the assertion that man's core is good. See?

The intrusion of the intellect at any point in this process is disastrous. Even a simple question, "Miss Jones, why exactly do you view man's core as essentially good?" will undo many months of exhibited behavior and reiterated precept. Notice, please, that the disaster lies *in the question*, not in the answer, although that would surely make things even worse. It is the asking of the question that marks the intrusion of the intellect, and it is no less devastating to humanisticism when the question is, as in fact it *usually* is, unspoken.

The inevitable collision of intellect and sentiment has even more frightful consequences. In a Sunday school it would be a simple demonstration either of dogmatism or typical grown-up hypocrisy, either of which children can easily recognize and shrug off. But classes in school, although they are in fact dedicated to the inculcation of beliefs, are often ostensibly devoted to some small work of the mind. In a biology class, therefore, intellectual inquiries are sometimes appropriate and sometimes not. The resultant confusion between what is knowable and what is not, and between statement of fact and assertion of belief, is usually sufficient to last any schoolchild for the rest of his life. And, for all the recitation of precepts and exhibitions of behavior, the lesson that he learns best is that his teachers could not make such distinctions either. Nor could *their* teachers.

To the incipient transpersonal teacher's view of man's core as good, we must also add, if we are teacher-trainers, the belief that "the locus of power and authority in one's life is within the individual." This curious proposition bristles with terms that are going to need very precise and narrow definitions if we are to find it credible. We will probably find that its very attractiveness as a sentiment will be drastically diminished when definitions are provided, and it is only in the absence of such definitions that anyone can recommend it as a major virtue. It becomes ludicrous when we imagine how the precept must be translated into practice in the teacher academy. Gum-chewing girls, still troubled by acne and addicted to movie magazines, will be persuaded that their chubby frames are loci of power and authority, notwithstanding the fact that their skills, the instruments of power, are minimal, and their knowledge, the root of authority, is meager. And, thus persuaded, they will go forth to exhibit the appropriate behaviors and recite the appropriate precepts in order to persuade poor and wretched children into the same sad delusion.

Now that we have given our would-be transpersonal teachers the belief, contrary to all evidence, that they are self-sufficient loci of power and authority and that man's core is inherently good, it remains only to see that they apply these values in "life situations" "with flexibility, and free of preconceptions of prejudice." Decisions, decisions. Well, what the hell. Let us by all means hold unalterably to that value about man's good core, until we flex it in a life situation, that is. On the other hand, though, can it be that that very belief, that is, the belief that we must be flexible about out beliefs, is one of those preconceptions and prejudices of which we must be free? Or can it be that the value out of which we flex our values is itself flexible, thus permitting us, in *certain* life situations, to be flexible enough not to be flexible and to free ourselves from that preconception about being free from preconceptions? Or can we just lie down and forget the whole damn thing? Such absurdities must always occur when the mouth runs off in the recitation of precepts couched in vague generalizations and undefined terms. But they do not trouble the educationistic humanisticists, who never seem to notice them. The important thing is that the precept *sounds* good. And it does — quite good enough, in fact, to be elevated into a principle of teacher education, where the disruptive questions of the intellect will never intrude.

I have been talking, of course, not of the specific program of any teacher-training academy but of Waterman's notions of "the personal characteristics related to transpersonal teaching." It may be, I admit, that there is somewhere in America a teacher academy that rejects such notions and also the notion that such notions have anything at all to do with effective teaching, but I don't think so. Waterman's "characteristics" are painfully familiar to anyone who has paid attention to the loudly proclaimed humanisticism of teacher-training. That's exactly the sort of thing they *all* say, and that they *all* champion as our only protection against the unbridled ruthlessness of intellectual discipline, also known as "excellence narrowly defined."

Excellence *broadly* defined, however, is a mild master. It

can be anything you like. And when broadly defined excellence is understood as the goal of a pious and humanisticist education, any sanctimonious amateur can fancy himself a teacher of anything at all. In the teacher academies this permits some startling but not at all uncommon courses, in which "appreciation" is the aim, in despite of knowledge.

A splendid example of the hokum thus generated came in the mail one day to the editorial offices of *The Underground Grammarian*. It was a mimeographed sheet, headed by one of those silly smiling faces and announcing a course in the Department of Educational Curriculum and Instruction at the University of Tennessee. The course, "The Existential Student," was for *seniors* and *graduate students*, and the "teacher," who billed himself as "Seminar Co-ordinator," was a certain Anand Kumar Malik. His powers must be unbounded; here's what he proposes:

> *OBJECTIVES*: Aim is to introduce the students in an informal situation to the major themes in existentialism and humanism; to make them aware of their basic inner freedom to lead an authentic life, to sing their own song, to dance their way through life, to relate themselves to themselves through self-understanding, to relate themselves to others through non-ego love, to accept their complete academic responsibility to their own growth and to enrich their own educational curriculum and life experiences. All in harmony with their basic responsibilities to others in the world.

There follows a description of the intended "Learning Experiences," on which I would like to comment, but cannot. My power of language is just not sufficient. Fortunately, however, a letter was enclosed with the announcement. It was printed in its entirety in *The Underground Grammarian* thus:

Song and Dance
in Tennessee

Dear Underground, I have been reading and studying your magazine for sometime and I truly do enjoy reading it. The onliest thing is, is that it is hard to study out what it means. At least always. I don't mean the Latin or whatever it is in the "headlines" which I can skip them anyway but it seems to me that folks up *North* make things out harder than they have to be some time and you could learn from us as well. You take Philosophy, as any one would call it a hard "subject" (but not in Knoxville) because you would want to read about the material dialects and the rational. Still, I think you would very seriously do it but end up finally with book learning that is alright in its place, however, life must go on as they say. You will see from the "enclosed" that Philosophy does not have to be hard, and not even Existentialism that is the hardest known Philosophy. It tells about Anand Kumar Malik and his course he is teaching called The Existential Student, and very well put by the "headline." "You are hereby invited to become no one but yourself." It gives a good feeling and the smiling face picture really gets the message across. Any one who could get themselves down to the University of Tennessee, in Knoxville this summer, could learn Existentialism *and* Humanism thrown in as the flyer says in only four (4) weeks in the dept. of Education, and that's what it is about after all. If I may give some quotes from the flier you will see that school can be fun, when the students learn "to sing their own song" and "to dance their way through life." It gives some selected writings too, and as I said there is not a thing wrong with book learning, but I have to admit that I don't recognize the names, except Elizabeth Lacey tells me that a friend of hers has a whole book of Philosophy by that Mr. Kahlil Gibran, or probably Prof. Gibran, and she says that he is "very good." (*Exact* quote!) They will have existential music and existential art slides, and "making your own existential painting." Best of all is they will "relate themselves to themselves through self-understanding" and that makes good sense if you ask me in my humble opinion. Maybe you shouldn't think school should be all that hard as you seem to think some times, because here is Mr. Malik whose not only an education teacher but he can teach Existentialism too, and he even lets the students figure up their grades so there won't be all that worry about flunking (failing.) Now that is the whole difference right there between the teachers and the others, and I bet you you won't find any cheerful smiling face picture drawn up at the top of any fancy medical school flyer. You take doctors and lawyers and even I hope you don't mind my saying so some of your college professors and you will find there is more than just one stuffed shirt between them. That is because all those "subjects" they study they make them so serious as though somebody's or other *life* depended on it. Life isn't all a rose colored glass, you know, and it is good to have faith that our school teachers can learn Existentialism and dance through it with a song in their heart nevertheless. I know you hate mistakes, so I looked up the hard words.

❖ ———————————————————————————————— ❖

To that breathtaking commentary I can add only a few ▸trivial footnotes: The writers whose "existential themes" are to be studied in four weeks are eighteen in number and range from Kierkegaard to Susan Polis Schutz, and include Carlos Castaneda as well as that celebrated existentialist, Kahlil Gibran. The students, who will, of course, determine their own grades, even as they sing their own songs and dance their own ways, will also keep "a small diary of . . . brief reactions to some existential ideas." Small. Brief. Some. And, naturally, *reactions*. Knowledge is not at issue. Each student is promised "an annotated bibliography on existentialism and humanism (for . . . continuous self-development after the seminar is over.)" Continuous self-development. As to how (or whether) existentialism and humanism are distinguished, I cannot say.

The ordinary citizen, contemplating such a juvenile parody of scholarship, is inclined to protect his sanity by assuming that such a course is a freakish anomaly. That, alas, cannot be so. This instructor, after all, is not an independent entrepreneur peddling self-help and uplift down at the Community Center on Tuesday evenings from seven to nine. This course is offered with the approval and connivance of his colleagues and co-conspirators in that Department of Educational Curriculum and Instruction and the entire administrative apparatus of the University of Tennessee. And that means, dear citizen, that not one of all those professors, committee members, chairmen, deans, vice-presidents, and who can say how many other functionaries, probably including legislative committees and the governor himself, had either enough knowledge or concern to suggest that the king was naked.

It would probably be a mistake to assume that the students enrolled in such a course were taken in by it, although there will be a few in any teacher-training program slow and gullible enough to mistake a small diary of brief reactions for the work of the mind. Students take those courses precisely *because* they are silly and easy, and you would do the same. Those credits are worth money. And on the other side of the transaction, the existence of such a course is also worth money — and professional respectability, and job security — to the one who teaches it and the system that permits it. That makes me suspicious. Although I think that I can understand why those seniors and graduate students, in search of certificates and raises, might glady take courses like "The Existential Student," I find it less easy to be tolerant of those who teach and sponsor them and of what can only be called the corporate complicity of the entire system of public education in America.

Furthermore, it is discouraging to notice that the graduates of our teachers' colleges, do *not*, as you might think, all forswear the nonsense to which they have been subjected once they have their certificates in hand. Or, if they do, they are remarkably secretive about it. In the kingdom of educationism, outspoken dissidents are rare. This is because those few who *do* dissent and shake off the childish humanisticism of their education courses have good reason to know that nothing can be done about anything. But it must also be because there are in any teachers' college enough of the slow and gullible to form a permanent population of committed humanisticists who will never change. I conclude that this must be so, for there is no other way to account for the existence and growing numbers of institutions like the Connecticut Teachers' Center for Humanistic Education, which was described thus in the pages of *The Underground Grammarian*:

The Black
Whole of Connecticut
"Mistah Kurtz—he transpersonalized."

The center cannot hold, you say? Poo. Come with us now, up some tranquil New England waterway leading to the uttermost ends of the earth and into the heart of an immense darkness. There, we will come at last to the Connecticut Teachers' Center for Humanistic Education, and it's holding very well indeed, thank you.

Dark humanistic shapes we will make out in the distance, flitting indistinctly against the gloomy border of the forest, and, chief among them, brooding over some inscrutable purpose, Emily, the Assistant Director. All we know of her is what we read in *Centering,* the Center's little newsletter. Here it is — *sic*:

> Emily has experience training in the areas of Bio-energetics, Psychosynthesis, Gestalt Therapy, Arica Psychocalesthenics, Yoga and Tai Chi. Emily has been a consultant to Connecticut Public Schools . . . in self-awareness training, confluent education, and organization development. . . . Emily is committed to working with individuals wholistically — facilitating the integration of their emotional, intellectual, physical and transpersonal aspects.

In the hush that falls suddenly upon the whole (or "hole,") sorrowful land, do remember that Emily is only the *Assistant* Director. What must *he* be, who can direct the labors of such an assistant? And whose heads are those, their transpersonal aspects hideously integrated on self-awareness training poles, that fence these murky precincts? They look so small.

We are lost, lost in an area. Is it the area of Psychosynthesis or the area of Tai Chi? Could we be in the neighborhood of Bio-energetics or even in the immediate environs of Arica Psycho-calesthenics? Who knows? They look so much alike. That's why we all need Assistant Directors, real *professionals* of education, with rigorous "experience training" in areas. Oh, what a mistake we made studying junk like geography when what we ought to have had was experience training somewhere in the area-awareness area. Now we just can't seem to facilitate the integration of *any* of our aspects. The horror, the horror.

We have, of course, no idea at all of what teachers *do* in a teachers' center, and we obviously never will, for the gravity of the Black Whole of Connecticut is so enormous that no light escapes. We can only guess, therefore, that teachers hie themselves there to have their Gestalten therapized in the lotus position, performing the while, quietly within the psyche, synthesizing calesthenics, whatever *those* may be, interspersed with an occasional aspect-integrating and bio-energizing round of Tai Chi, perhaps a confluent form of Parcheesi for individuals. That would explain a lot.

That's all we can tell you. Like that other cryptic screed, our source gave "no practical hints to interpret [or even to understand] the magic current of its phrases . . . unless a kind of note . . . scrawled evidently much later, may be regarded as the exposition of a method," or, at least, of a course in methodology. "It was very simple, and at the end of that moving appeal to every altruistic sentiment it blazed . . . luminous and terrifying, like a flash of lightning in a serene sky: 'Excruciate the brats!' " And that, of course, would explain *everything*.

Maybe I'm wrong. Maybe it isn't out of cynicism but something worse that students in teachers' colleges take courses in self-relating through life experiences. Maybe it's folly. Maybe stupidity. Maybe it's just the paralysis of the mind that may well befall anyone who has taken enough of such courses and listened to such cant and endured, bored and thus uncritical, the foolish circular arguments, generalizations, and non sequiturs of educationistic vaporizing. The teachers who frequent that Connecticut Teachers' Center for Humanistic Education, and there must be some, perhaps many, go there of their own free will. They must *want* Psychosynthesis and Tai Chi. They must want to be worked with "wholistically" in the cause of the facilitation of the integration of their aspects. And the educationist bureaucrats who take our money for the support of the Connecticut Teachers' Center for Humanistic Education must want the teachers to want such things. And the schools must have wanted to consult with Emily, again at our expense, on self-awareness training and organization development. In a world where all of that is not only possible but even usual, cynicism seems a refreshing virtue.

But it is precisely in such a climate, where self-help facilitations and puerile popularizations can blossom, that the pseudo-science and pseudo-religion of educationism can spread and flourish. In a climate of hard knowledge and rational analysis such flamboyant weeds would wither and die in a season. But that won't happen. To their unique blend of the illogical and the sentimental, the educationists have added the techniques of a man to whom they owe far more than they do to Horace Mann, or John Dewey, or even Wundt, poor Wundt. The guiding spirit of the *methods* of educationism, if not the ideology, is, of course, Dale Carnegie.

The
Pygmies' Revenge

*P*eter's well-known Principle was obviously discovered by a man who knew nothing at all about schools. In schools it just isn't true that the people who can actually do their jobs get promoted until they find themselves, at last and forever, in the jobs they can't do. This is because the most difficult and demanding jobs in education are what industry calls "entry-level positions," teaching in classrooms. That's the bottom rung of the school ladder, and there are many people who just can't do that work. It isn't, in itself, very difficult work; all it takes is intelligence, diligence, talent, and a little bit of luck. Those who have some of the first three, however, often run clean out of the fourth when they start taking education courses and start worrying more about enhancing their personological variables than about collecting more knowledge. (Furthermore, teaching obviously has to be done in a school, and many of our schools, after decades of eschewing "mere information" in the cause of "worthy citizenship," have turned into lawless encampments of armed barbarians where no one can teach and no

one can learn.) Those who are short on intelligence, diligence, and talent, however, find their luck much improved
by the fact that the teachers' colleges are designed for just
such people.

Thus, partly because so many have incompetence thrust
upon them, and partly because so many are born to incompetence, in every faculty there will be people who just can't
handle the entry-level position. In industry, or even in a
fast-food restaurant, they would be washed out; but we don't
do that kind of thing in the schools, especially since public
school teaching is more and more used by government as a
jobs program for the less able. In the schools, those who
cannot do the work at the lowest rank are simply promoted
into higher ranks. Weirdly enough, given the nature of the
educational enterprise, this makes perfect sense.

In those realms where the Peter Principle prevails, it is
often true that higher rank and higher pay do go along with
harder work. In the schools, where there *is* no harder work
than teaching in a classroom, exactly the opposite is true.
In fact, it is not at all absurd to imagine a perfectly splendid
school in which there are only teachers and one clever and
industrious handyman who can also type. On the other hand,
think for a moment about the school toward which, as all
the statistics suggest, we might be moving, a school made up
almost entirely of administrators and their own "support
services." (They usually call them that.) In such a school we
would see clearly what we now can see only darkly, through
the frosted glass of governmental mandate and educationistic
dogma: that almost all of the work done by those above the
rank of teacher is contrived so that there may be more
workers. Thus it is that so much of the administrative work

done in schools is intended not to *do work*, as a physicist would use the term, but to occupy time and justify the existence of some administrative post.

It turns out, not surprisingly therefore, that the mindless and inflated jargon, superbly suited to the darkening of logic and the interminable belaboring of the obvious, is exactly the language that an educationistic administrator needs in order to conceal the fact that the work he does simply doesn't need doing. If you want to rise in the school business, you have to master the lingo. This is another reason why good teachers don't become principals and superintendents: The very attributes that make them good teachers also make it impossible for them to talk about experiential remediation enhancement strategies with straight faces. And if there is one attribute a principal or superintendent needs, it's a perfectly straight face. You have to believe. Solemnly.

When those who can't teach want to improve themselves by becoming supervisors of those who *can* teach, they must go through, once again, the strait gate of the teachers' college. Outside of that church, there is no salvation. They must return, perhaps on Monday and Thursday evenings, to the study, if that's the word, of such arcana as Curriculum Development and Supervision, Career and Guidance Counseling, and Educational Administration/Management. Since there is little to be learned about such matters, the courses are easy, requiring mostly the ability to tolerate ponderous recitations of the trivial and obvious and a mind just weak enough to fall without a struggle into an habitual inanity in language. These are the very proclivities that have made the poorer teachers what they are, so there is no shortage of suitable candidates for graduate study in the schools of education. While the steady stream of aspirants to lofty (non-teaching) rank assures perpetual public funding for the teachers' colleges and pleasant, permanent employment for professors of education, it has some even more unhappy consequences. It assures that the anti-intellectual climate of the public high schools will prevail in the colleges and universities as well. Except for the uncharacteristically depraved, professors of chemistry or history, or of any traditional discipline with a concrete and growing body of knowledge, simply don't *want* to do the boring and empty work of administration. They gladly leave that to the educationists and other nonacademic arrivistes in higher education, who gladly take it. Thus it comes to pass that in most of our colleges and universities policy decisions about academic matters are regularly made by direct descendants of the Commission on the Reorganization of Secondary Education, to whom intellectual discipline and mere information are pesky impediments to worthy ethical character and right emotional response.

The work of school administration, therefore, usually has two typical attributes: Because it must justify the very existence of school administration, it must seem time-consuming and difficult. Because it is an instrument of educationistic ideology, it must be "humanistic" and "democratic," as the educationists understand those terms, which is to say emotional and collective rather than coldly knowledgeable and authoritarian. You can recognize in the typical administrative committee, therefore, a long-trouser version of the social studies class envisioned in *Cardinal Principles*, where it is imagined that ignorant but right-feeling children will corporately hatch out wisdom.

Here, from the pages of *The Underground Grammarian*, is an example of how the administrative work of an institution of higher education is actually done:

Ask a Stupid Question . . .

Glassboro has so many low-ranking, junior administrators that it's hard to find them useful work. We don't even try, in fact; we just find them things to play with.

George Wildman and Robert Harris are co-chairmen of the Task Force on Recruitment, Retention, and Image. We don't know how they produce their prose — whether by one as told to the other or by taking turns word by word — but here's how it comes out:

> In the first two sessions of the Task Force, the group explored the task facing them. Discussion ensued during these sessions concerning the goals and objectives to be accomplished. The Committee began the task of gathering supporting data by virtue of reports supplied by the offices of Admissions, Counseling, and the Registrar. Considerable time was spent attempting to define terminology as a basis for functioning, and much thought was given in an attempt to identify some of the major concerns which the Task Force would be facing in its work.

The first, second, and fourth sentences of that paragraph say the same thing, although the fourth *does* add that bit about defining "terminology [terms?] as a basis for functioning." The third sentence actually has its own thing to say, but only that they "began the task of gathering." Does that mean that they began gathering or that they began getting ready to gather? This sentence also uses "by virtue of" as though it meant "from." Never ask a junior administrator to say something straight out. He'd rather be knocked flat in an airport by O. J. Simpson. (Good idea.)

Since the combined salaries of the twenty members of this Task Force must be more than half a million dollars a year, we're glad to report that their labor has had some results. As early as their second meeting, they divided themselves into three "interest-area subcommittees" (shouldn't that be sub–Task Forces or Task Forcelets?), one each for Recruitment, Retention, and Image.

They did more. Each interest area subcommittee undertook to "define its term."

Now you would think that any fool could define *recruitment, retention,* and even *image,* although why that should be necessary is not clear. We have to guess that many members of the Task Force were unacquainted with those words and needed remediational input.

Discussion ensued by virtue of input, and tasks were explored. Thought was given in an attempt, and time was spent attempting.

By the next meeting, each "interest-area" subcommittee had defined "its term." Here's what they found — as a basis for functioning:

recruitment: the institution's philosophy and procedures by which we attempt to attract students to continue their education . . .

retention: the ability of the college to hold students who are pursuing a degree program (B.A., M.A., including certification).

image: the reflection of reality and substance.

 ————————————————————————————

The language of these administrators is symbolic, as language always is, although in this case not consciously symbolic. They do on the page exactly what they do in their jobs. They say over and over again a thing that needs no saying in the first place. They set themselves, at public expense, to the silly task of defining, in *groups* no less, terms (or, as they prefer, terminology) that need no defining. If their labors were successful, they would learn at great expense of time and money what any thoughtful person could have told them at their first meeting, and they will inevitably propose the obvious. They will urge more recruitment and retention along with image-enhancement.

It is important for the ordinary citizen to realize that such committees, through whose agency almost everything is done in Academe, are not composed entirely of administrators. There will always be some members who are only incipient administrators making themselves useful and noteworthy, some junior professors bucking for promotion and not at all reluctant to be parties to a lengthy and arduous reinvention of the wheel, and other faculty members somewhat less than passionately devoted to their chosen disciplines. The latter, of course, are usually from an education department, where a passionate devotion to discipline is precluded not only by the questionable nature and content of what is taught but by the traditional animosity to discipline itself.

If you can assemble enough such people and assign them an especially ambiguous errand, neither of which is at all difficult in a school, you can easily devise an educationistic enterprise that can go on, literally, forever:

 The Future Lies Ahead!

Early in the Fall, the Needs Assessment Task Force was asked to study the process of Academic Planning as it presently exists at Southwest Texas State University and determine whether we should implement a different process. (From the works of Joseph Caputo, VP for AcAff.)

As the time for dinner approaches, the standard American amateur looks in the refrigerator. He notices some food. He takes some of it out and cooks it. Then he eats it. It's so crude; any savage could do it. Here in Academe, we are "professionals," and we have better ways of doing things.

First we establish a committee to consider whether or not there should *be* any dinner, and, if so, whether or not it should actually be eaten, and, if again so, where, and when, and by whom. Then we form a subcommittee to decide what, if anything, to cook, and how. Now we discover that we need a study group to consider whether or not dinner-planning is, in fact, all that simple, and to establish its parameters and to explore the implications of fiscal, curricular, and societal restraints that may be perceived as existing. Or maybe not. But the study group cannot do its work until we have definitive findings from the Needs Assessment Task Force, which is "to study the process of Academic Planning as it presently exists . . . and determine whether we should implement a different process."

The Needs Assessment Task Force down at Southwest Texas State University, where the squirrels *also* rush around the brush, has done its work. Here's some of it:

> An Academic Planning Model must involve a futures planning component. Goals should be set for some time in the future. These goals should be translated into shorter-term objectives for which the degree of detail and concreteness varies inversely with the lead time. There should also be reasonable suspense dates for implementation of plans and a definitive methodology for evaluation and feedback. The interfacing of long-term . . . and short-term planning should result.

So, you thought that only a herd of nerds would set themselves to wondering whether or not to plan how to plan, eh? No siree! It takes some of the sharpest thinkers in Academe to discover and announce that plans are about the "future," not the past!

They're even smart enough to call for the involvement of a component, which would never occur to an ordinary human being, and a definitive methodology, where any simpleminded taxpayer would have settled for a mere method.

That's not all, of course. The Task Forcers also urge "update features," prudently left unspecified so that yet another task can be forced on yet another task force, and warn against the "counterproductive hurdle," the worst kind. One of their main conclusions, solemnly pronounced, probably after much deliberation and searching of heart, is that an Academic Planning Model (they always capitalize it) should actually *work,* or, as they put it, "be functional." They further opine, cutting right to the bone, that any plan that will work, will in fact work: "Any Academic Planning Model to be considered . . . would positively impact [wham!] our decision-making process to the extent that it accomplishes its designed purpose."

To proclaim the obvious in language that is odious is, of course, the regular practice of the educationists, who love to serve on task forces (they put that kind of stuff in their résumés and grant applications), and have no moral or intellectual objections to writing at length about nothing. However, at least one member of this task force was *not* an educationist, but an *agent provocateur* and a subtle ironist. On his backward colleagues he foisted the one sentence that says it all: "An Academic Planning process must not become viewed by the participants as activity to be finished so that they may return to the real business of the university."

 ————————————————————————————————

Then again, to be sure, the revelation of that last sentence may have been due simply to ineptitude. But the revelation is a true one, for, as far as the educationist is concerned, "the real business of the university" is not what you probably think.

For years, I have been looking around for the key, the master metaphor, the one striking analogy that would clarify and dramatize the nature of our schools. They are, of course, something like the asylum where the inmates have taken over, but that doesn't do the whole job. They are more like some island nation in which the traditional, mild, but inefficient governance once exercised by a genteel but effete and distracted aristocracy has been taken over, without any bloodshed at all, by bands of persistent pygmies from the unexplored interior. The less than worldly aristocrats, far more interested in watching for comets and collecting Lepidoptera than in zoning rules and customs control, were not displeased to accede when the pygmies drifted in and offered to do all the hard work. It seemed such a good idea at the time, but by now the pygmies are in charge of everything, and the bemused aristocrats, whose ancestral estates have been converted to miniature golf courses, find that they are sipping their soup out of very small spoons.

But that metaphor isn't enough either, for it does not provide a place for the only slightly rationalized vengefulness that characterizes the educationists' almost complete governance of what was once an academic and intellectual confederation of semiautonomous principalities. We might do better to think of Bolsheviks in the Winter Palace, or the moneychangers in the temple who have it in mind not only to do a flourishing business but to preach the doctrine as well, thus ensuring that business will always flourish. I think that latter analogy especially good, but not very entertaining. The former, however, while even less entertaining, may be even better, for educationism is in fact an ideological collectivism devoted to social change through institutionalized thought control, but of that more later.

Perhaps the best metaphor, although unfortunately the nastiest, is that of racism. If we could divide the world of schools roughly, and it would be very roughly at best, into two "races," the academicians and the educationists, we would find some useful analogies. The educationists, although long released from slavery, have indubitably been treated like second-class citizens and kept in the ghettos. From the point of view of the academicians, the department of education, where not even the educationists have been able to identify a concrete body of knowledge out of which to make a "subject," is as much a ghetto as any local public school. The educationists, although they eagerly do the scutwork of administration, have never been admitted into the society of the "learned," and they have had to make their own sub-society complete with its own sub–Phi Beta Kappa and countless sub-journals of sub-scholarship. (It is an interesting irony that the learned journals of literary criticism, for example, are often as pretentiously impenetrable as anything you can find in any one of those apparently countless journals of educationistic research into perceived personological variables, but the diction is more noble and the verbs almost always agree with the subjects.) In faculty dining rooms all over the country, historians and biologists and professors of Renaissance literature happily lunch together, but the educationists usually keep to themselves. The very degrees that educationists award one another are held to be inferior to the degrees that the academicians award one another. Although the traditional "original contribution to scholarship" expected of the academic doctoral dissertation is often ludicrously picayune, the dissertation in education, often nothing more than a report on the results of some questionnaire, ordinarily deals with either the obvious, like the conclusion that children who want to learn will learn more than those who don't; or the trivial, like the mechanics of pencil distribution; or the utterly ineffable, like the perceived personological existential variables. Furthermore, the doctorate in education almost never requires that signal cachet of the learned scholar, competence in foreign languages. This often cited distinction is enough by itself to "prove" to the academicians the innate inferiority of the race of educationists.

The prejudice is real, and the educationists, naturally, resent it. Much of what they do, therefore, can be understood as an expectably hostile thirst for revenge. *Cardinal Principles* is only superficially a plan for secondary education; it is essentially a *Summa contra gentiles*, a stick-it-to-the-intellectuals manifesto. The pronouncements of *Cardinal Principles* must be read in two ways.

Consider, for example, the proposition that a disciplined academic study of literature, whatever that might mean, precludes "right emotional response." On the one hand, that shows the "humane" intention to provide students with the "best" that literature has to offer, certain feelings, presumably good to have. It asserts, and who would deny, that the pity and terror of tragedy will strike even those who are utterly ignorant of the textual variants, although it also provides the possibility that pity or terror might not be included among the "right" emotional responses. On the other hand, it makes clear that the "teachers" of literature in the secondary schools can do *their* jobs without having to go through all that disciplined scholarship by which those lofty academicians make their livings. From that notion it is not far to the next, to wit, that the academicians are in fact *preventing* right emotional response with their footnotes and critical editions and that the only path to right emotional response is the deliberate neglect of such things. With the next step we can see that ignorance is better than knowledge, an idea singularly attractive to those who have not *read* any of the footnotes or critical editions.

The dream of putting down the scornful mighty from their chairs also informs another cardinal tenet of educationism: the notion widely held in the teacher academies that all a teacher needs is training in how to teach, with which he can teach anything at all, perhaps with a little boning up. Thus it is that the high school social studies teacher, already inoculated against the dehumanizing effects of the "mere information" associated with the disciplined study of history, can readily be retreaded into a teacher of English. After all, we all speak English, don't we? In any case, what is important is not what a teacher knows but how he relates to the students. Such ideas are impossible where academic subjects are held important in themselves, but where they are seen only as the devices by which to generate feelings it is inevitable that existentialism (*and* humanism, in the same package deal) boils down to singing your own song and dancing your way through life in a two-week summer session.

Such Jack-of-all-tradesism, although long a regular practice in the public schools, is a little harder to get away with in colleges and universities. But *just* a little. Anand Kumar Malik, you must have noticed, seems to have had no trouble at all in setting up shop as a teacher of philosophy and even of painting at the same time. Here we can see the mighty consequences of the fact that educationists are eager to serve on committees and to undertake the dull labors of administration. Without powerful co-conspirators in the superstructure at the University of Tennessee, Malik would have been laughed off the campus and sent to sing and dance for a much smaller supper in the Thursday evening class at the YMCA.

It probably isn't exactly true that we become what we hate. It seems more likely that we become a parody of what we hate. Certainly the oppressed and scorned educationists, driven in part by oppression and scorn to denigrate the very intellectual powers they are said to lack, are pathetically eager nevertheless to lay claim to those powers for themselves, and also to the expertise that such powers can provide. Thus they put themselves forth as — well, not exactly professors of philosophy, but at least as easy professors of easy philosophy. Students like that, of course, but it makes professors of philosophy glum.

Given the principle that any subject matter is a useful device for the generation of socially desirable feeling, and given also the fact that policymaking in colleges and universities has been conceded to the educationists who proclaim that given principle, it follows that "higher" education will have its analogues of the phys. ed. teacher who takes over when the biology teacher gets pregnant, of course. But it *also* follows, even more ominously, that there is really no need for a biology teacher in the first place. And in college, where the biology teacher is firmly entrenched in tradition and tenure, it further follows that the study of biology itself might just as well be replaced with something else, something that can be "taught" by one who knows little of biology but who has been trained as a teacher and whose eye is on not the biology itself but on whatever worthy attitudes that may, or should, arise from the study of biology. Since those attitudes *are* the worth of the study, why bother with the study when one can jump right into the attitudes?

Here is an example of exactly such a leap of faith, which legitimizes a startling educationistic Anschluss of a host of traditional and concretely identifiable academic studies:

 ## Long Underdue

The Department of Foundations of Education has proposed a workshop in "intercultural education" to tack three more hours onto a course in the same thing, if that *is* a thing. From reading the proposal, we guess that both course and workshop call for lots of "relating" and "interacting," and, naturally, "problem-solving," with "foci on direct field experience" and "working on real school or/and community problems." (That sure beats indirect field experience and fake problems, but these folk are into "professional" matters, not amateur dabbling like math or history.) As far as we can tell, there will be no study of any identifiable body of knowledge, just rapping, preferably with someone who says *Mama mia!* now and then.

This workshop is not expected to have results; it anticipates "outcomes," outcomes of some "nature." One anticipated outcome is:

> of the nature of . . . development of ability to anticipate factors likely to influence proposals for changes in human relations . . .

What this means, of course, is that they hope the student will be informed, rational, and prudent. So hope we all; but to suggest that there are forms of rationality and prudence specifically germane to "intercultural relations" is fatuous. To suggest further that someone knows how to instill those virtues is patently absurd, if not mendacious. Who is rational and prudent needs no workshop to teach him how to be rational and prudent about Bulgarians any more than a man who can find the diameter of a circle needs to be schooled in the methodology of finding the diameter of a pizza; and who is neither prudent nor rational will scarcely be helped through chatting with Bulgarians. Furthermore, who would become knowledgeable about Bulgarians will do better to study their history or language or literature than to pursue

> [d]evelopment of ability to apply selected tools or procedures for analyzing, assessing, and surveying school and/or community provisions for intercultural education.

And how will students show that they have (get? interact with? what?) these outcomes? The proposal looks for "taped evidence of interaction with other cultures" (they probably mean a *person* from another culture), "oral presentations that exemplify good intercultural education practices," "peer performance assessments," "records of participation" (in what, would you guess?), and even "practical written tools" (try to figure *that* one out).

We must put aside small questions (how, for instance, is a good intercultural education practice different from other good education practices?) to explore the central question: What, exactly, *is* the subject matter here? Is it information about diverse cultures? *That* is available — inescapable, in fact — in the study of anthropology, art, economics, geography, history, language, literature, philosophy, religion, and many other traditional disciplines. Is this the study of the collisions of cultures and their effects upon one another? Ditto. Is this a study of tolerance and love?

The proposers cannot intend either of the first two, for if they do, there is no need to propose anything. Let's hope they don't mean that third possibility. There must be *some* limits to what they can teach.

If intercultural education is in truth some new subject matter not yet widely known, it must have been described *somewhere* in clear English and with concrete reference to things in the real world. We deserve to hear such a description, since the language of the proposal tells us little (that's often the aim of this kind of jargon) and makes us suspect much.

We must in fairness say that the proposal has been given comprehensive, penetrating scrutiny and analysis by the very Dean of Professional Studies, so it seems only honest to print *her* commentary — in full:

A good idea — long overdue.

❖ ——————————————————————————— ❖

The background of that proposal is instructive: In the State of New Jersey, as in many other states, students in teacher-training programs are required to have some instruction in what is generally called the "appreciation" of other cultures. This seems to be all the more important as the public schools, especially in the cities, fill up with children of recently arrived immigrants from many different lands. I say that it "seems" important, because I'm not sure that it is really necessary to "appreciate" Bulgarian culture, whatever that means, in order to teach arithmetic to children whose parents came from Bulgaria, although it would obviously do a math teacher no harm to have *knowledge* about Bulgarian culture. But the mandate, in any case, is not for knowledge. The incipient teacher is to *appreciate* other cultures so that he can *relate* and *interact*.

Here we see again — we see it everywhere — the shadow

of *Cardinal Principles*. Knowledge, generally a matter of mere information, is untrustworthy as a generator of right response, so that intercultural appreciation can be taught through learning some folk dances and sampling the traditional cookies of many lands. But it *must* be taught, for those who award teaching certificates require it. They require it because their cousins in the teacher academies, whose enrollments are falling, need some more required courses with which to justify their continued employment. In the same cause, and with the great weight of the tradition of *Cardinal Principles*, the teacher-trainers must hold that such academic studies as anthropology, history, literature, or language can *not* provide a worthy appreciation of other cultures. Since the teacher-trainers, and the certifiers, and the managers and bureaucrats of entire systems of state education are all from the same litter, and since legislators all have more important things than education to think about, especially in New Jersey, where someone has to pay attention to casinos, basic minimum intercultural appreciation speedily becomes the law of the land. And the professors of education who get to "teach" it have assured their continued employment and proved yet again that a teacher can teach anything, anything at all.

Educationists can say that, of course, only when "anything" means "anything that should be taught," in the system of worthiness enunciated in *Cardinal Principles*, and when "taught" means "produced as a response to stimulus," as defined in the methodology of behavior modification. You will notice that the state-supported monopoly in intercultural education does *not* concede that a professor of anthropology can teach "the appreciation of other cultures." Far from it, he is all too likely to teach mere information, which may or may not lead to what *should* be taught, appreciation, the worthy response.

That's why the word "appreciation" is so important both in *Cardinal Principles* and in all educationistic theorizing thereafter. First, it sounds good. Who can be against it? More important, it is a code word with which to indicate, without having to be concrete and specific, any or all of the "worthy" attributes that we may expect as the student outcomes of anything that is done in school, however trivial or trendy. In one sense, "appreciation" is familiar to anyone who has been through "Music Appreciation," a course that usually does *not* require any study or knowledge of harmony, counterpoint, or even the classification of elementary forms, although it often does provide uplifting or entertaining vignettes from the lives of composers. In another and far more important sense, the meaning of "appreciation" is what is embedded in the notion that when we have learned some Bulgarian folk dances we will better "appreciate" Bulgarian culture, and that that will be good. "Appreciation" seems to be used to suggest an amiable tolerance of that which someone thinks we *ought* to tolerate but probably wouldn't if we were left alone.

A student outcome of the order of appreciation has another tremendous value in an anti-intellectual education: No one can measure it. No one can measure "right emotional response" or "worthy ethical character" either. The value of such student outcomes is in fact double. They make it impossible to check up on the effectiveness of a curriculum, and they permit the bogus "research" of educationistic theorizing, in which such things as existentiality and commitment to the goodness of man at his core are put forth as measurable quantities. Who is to say, after all, exactly which students, and with what ardor, are indeed singing their own songs and dancing their ways through life after two weeks of harmony and small-group discussions at the University of Tennessee? Unfortunately, someone probably *will* undertake to do just that, perhaps the very chappie who told us all about the "values, attitudes, and teaching philosophy pertinent to transpersonally oriented non-public school teachers."

The Student Outcomes Principle (it seems to deserve capitals) is the Prime Mover of American education. It is our equivalent of the Death of God, after which everything is permitted. It arises inevitably from the intersection of that sentimental humanisticism that has made the schools into virtue-nurseries where guards patrol the corridors, and the iron law of behavior modification that has made them laboratories where all the experiments fail. But that's all right. As schools, and consequently the rest of society, become more anarchic, the educationists can point to an ever greater need for the inculcation of values, and every failed experiment makes room for new devils in the guise of faddish innovations.

But the Student Outcomes Principle has brought us even worse abominations than the fads and gimmicks that have been tripping over each other's heels for the last sixty years. Since the proponents of that principle have become the makers of policy at all levels of public education, they have been able to refashion even the most traditional courses of study into exercises in the inculcation of right emotional response and the clarification of values. Such was proposed, of course, in *Cardinal Principles* and in some cases easily effected by the ouster of history for the sake of social studies, for instance, in which the especially civic virtues, whatever they happen to be at any given time, are fostered by idle gossip about current events and some ill-informed generalizations about remote tribes.

The process, however, has only *begun* when social studies are implanted in the secondary public schools. Imagine what happens thereafter: At first, of course, the history teachers must be the social studies teachers. The less committed they are to the traditional study of history, the more likely they are to welcome this opportunity to escape the tyranny of mere information and develop instead an "appreciation and . . . a clear conception of right relations." History itself now becomes nothing more than *a* social study, and by no means *primus inter pares* but rather an aging and demanding relative less and less acceptable in a rapidly growing family of trendy issues. The next generation of social studies teachers cannot be students of history, or certainly not *merely* students of history. This means that whatever is to be done in the high schools in the name of social studies must also be done in the teachers' colleges where the social studies teachers are to learn their trade. The professors of such things as history and economics, therefore, have to be reeducated. They must welcome into partnership the sociologists, who are cousins to the educationists both in language and ideology, and learn to appreciate the priority of values over mere information. This is done in the name of "meeting the needs of the students," which is another way of expressing the Student Outcomes Principle, and which can have any practical effect you please depending only on the "needs" chosen.

Imagine that you are a bright young history scholar who has become an instructor in a college where there is a school of teacher education. After a year or two of teaching the basic freshman course in Western Civilization, which is already a social studies course, devoted to a little bit of everything and anything that probably ought to be appreciated, you discover that you would like to spend more time in teaching about the Renaissance in Italy, a body of knowledge in which you are especially well informed. Since the history department is small and offers no course in the Italian Renaissance, you write a description and a syllabus and send off a course proposal to the curriculum committee, with the blessing of your fellow history professors, who believe that the Italian Renaissance is worth studying.

Now your proposal comes before the curriculum committee, where the educationists and would-be administrators are serving with gladness and where the rules and procedures, as well as the ideology, have long been established by others of their kind. When they look at your proposal, they do not think about the intrinsic value of the study of the Renaissance in Italy, they ask rather about the projected student outcomes and the measurable behavioral objectives. They don't really want to hear what you could probably tell them: that those who study the Italian Renaissance can come to have knowledge. They want to know what kind of people your students will become, what they will appreciate, and whether they will be able to relate the Renaissance in Italy to the goals of self-fulfillment. In short, they will want to know, although the chances are good that no single member of the curriculum committee has ever heard of *Cardinal Principles*, exactly what it is that makes your course "worthy" in spite of its distinctly academic taint.

In response, you can, of course, lie. You can trump up some noble and plausible outcomes and objectives. That would probably work, for it is standard practice in any case, especially in the courses in education, and your interlocutors would be receptive to loose talk about appreciation of cultural heritage and the relating of self to self and others both as groups and individuals. You can say such things about the study of anything or even about dabbling in anything, cookery or karate, for that matter. But such a maneuver has, for *you* at least, two nasty consequences. First, you become either a fool or a liar. You may actually come to believe your concoctions, in which case you become a fool, but you can escape folly only by knowing yourself a liar, or, as we in the academic world prefer, a pragmatist. You lie in good cause, naturally, and in the company of all the other pragmatists who devise student outcomes and behavioral objectives in order to get past the curriculum committee, but still you lie. Lying and scholarship cannot live together, but lying and indoctrination are made for each other. Where scholarship is not practiced for its own sake but only in the service of doctrine, everybody has to lie — or be a fool — and your proposed course in Renaissance Italy must be put forth only as a means to some higher (and socially more acceptable) end than the mere learning of some knowledge.

And there is the other nasty consequence. If you do lie and cook up some lovely student outcomes and behavioral objectives that can justify the study of the Italian Renaissance, you explicitly admit that the higher end is more important than the means, since the latter can be justified only because of the former. That being so, your cunningly devised outcomes and objectives, which sound amazingly like the outcomes and objectives of many other courses, are obviously ends that might be achieved by many other means.

Thus, whatever it is that makes your proposed course "worthy" also makes it unnecessary. But that fact doesn't doom your proposed course, although it may doom *you*. If you have lied well enough, your course will be approved, since the continuous multiplication of courses is a profitable practice in any case, because it is now an admission by a humbled elitist academic that disciplined study is no more than a means to certain student outcomes. And once you have admitted that, you have become a de facto educationist. If you are willing to teach the history of the Renaissance in Italy as a way of engendering right appreciation of a cultural heritage and an exercise in relating self to self and others, then you must admit the academic validity of any other course, including cookery, that can make the same claims. You must also admit that students might just as well take cookery as your history course, for the student outcomes are the same. And, worse yet, you may someday have to admit, since, by your own confession, knowledge, or mere information, is *not* in fact the main point of your course, that it could just as well be taught by someone who is *not* a scholar of the Renaissance in Italy. And that is why it is that educationists can find permanent work teaching ten-cent-store equivalents of anything in the catalog, and, far worse, why once-serious scholars can end up doing the same thing without even knowing it.

It is interesting to notice that there are some studies that are by nature resistant to this process, and even more interesting to discover that they are the very studies where the failures of public education are most obvious. No amount of prattle about "right emotional response" to literature can for long disguise the fact that students can't read literature, and worthy appreciation of the logic of mathematics rarely assures the ability to cipher. The failure of the schools to teach these and other "fundamental processes" briefly mentioned and dismissed in *Cardinal Principles* is nowadays well known, but we have not yet given enough thought to the *reason* for that failure. It is not sufficient, although it is more and more true, to say that the children cannot read and write and cipher because their teachers cannot read and write and cipher. That just puts the question off one more step and leaves us to wonder how the teachers came to suffer that disability. The answer is to be found in that intellectual miasma emitted by the Student Outcomes Principle, which always holds, remember, that the truly desirable outcomes of any study at all are attitudes or values of some sort and not mere skill or information. Because they insist on teaching what is unteachable, educationists must denigrate the teaching of what *is* teachable. Where the pygmies rule, everybody else has to crouch.

Having seized power from the wicked elitists, the pygmy educationists are always busy stamping out vestiges of the old régime and its discredited ideals and practices. If you want to make an educationist wince, all you have to do is cite some "facts and dates," which you could know only as the result of "rote learning." Such things are all characterized in *Cardinal Principles* as notorious impediments to the true goals of education. They are not only elitist but oppressive and antidemocratic as well, and it may even be that a detailed knowledge of the constitution, for instance, would prevent the proper appreciation of our institutions and their values. It follows inevitably that those studies that depend heavily on memorization, mere "rote learning," will be given very short shrift indeed in our schools and the same in our teacher academies. Just as the instructor of Renaissance Italian history forswears himself by proposing anything other than knowledge as the goal of study, the educationist forswears himself and all that he stands for in permitting the suggestion that the goal of study is just knowledge. Thus it is that the educationists just don't know what to do with subjects that cannot, like history or literature, for example, be diluted for the sake of noncognitive student outcomes. And when they can't dilute a subject, they just neglect it.

It is for that reason, in fact, that along with reading and writing and ciphering, another equally "basic" study has fallen out of favor in the schools, and that is the study of foreign languages. We make a virtue of ignorance and sloth by claiming that a distaste for foreign languages is an American attribute, and while perhaps lamentable, nevertheless a tribute to the tough independence of our pioneer forebears. Many of those forebears, however, obviously saw the knowledge of other languages as an elementary part of an education and nothing more esoteric than literacy itself. Our supposed distaste for foreign language has in fact been fabricated in the schools. Foreign language study is not mentioned in *Cardinal Principles*, and it must be precisely what is *excluded* when that document, asserting that the language skills of elementary school children are "not yet sufficient," points out that "this is particularly true of the mother tongue." And foreign language is, no doubt, one of those "provisions" that might be made for "those having distinctively academic interests and needs." What we think of now as the lack of interest in foreign languages, and the obvious and unpleasant social and economic effects of that lack, to say nothing of the intellectual, is simply the inevitable consequence of the anti-intellectual educationism that informed *Cardinal Principles.*

The ideological distortion that can twist the study of literature into the inculcation of right emotional response just won't work with the study of irregular verbs. And, while any half-baked teacher of social studies can peddle appreciation of institutions without any tiresome concern for facts and dates, a teacher of German actually has to know the prepositions that take the dative. Furthermore, the results of foreign language study, and thus perhaps even the efficacy of teaching, can be measured concretely and objectively. Either you have learned those prepositions, and "by rote" at that, or you haven't. The Student Outcomes Principle just won't stretch far enough to cover the study of foreign languages. The only thing left is neglect, which is made all the more acceptable by the implication, already visible in *Cardinal Principles,* that a knowledge of French or — God forbid! — Greek is an esoteric dabbling in the arcane and nothing more than an antiquated social adornment suitable only for elitists. (Indeed, something very much like that same judgment is nowadays made of expertise in "the mother tongue" as well, which makes it much easier to apply the Student Outcomes Principle to the study of reading and writing English, where creativity and self-expression are held more important than spelling and punctuation, mere "rote learning.")

Because of the educationistic hegemony in public "higher" education, which is more often than not a clumsy apparatus built around a teacher-training academy, the neglect of foreign language study is just as common in the colleges as in the high schools. The neglect of foreign language, in fact, is a splendid case in point out of which to show that whatever happens in the realm of educationism must eventually have an effect not only everywhere in education itself but everywhere in our society.

As foreign languages are less and less studied in the public schools, fewer and fewer language teachers are needed, and enrollments decline in foreign language departments in teachers' colleges. As enrollments decline, the numbers of language professors decline, and some languages disappear entirely from the curriculum. That's not bad; it's good. It justifies still further neglect in the high schools, where, when the last old Latin teacher finally retires, the principal can replace her with an auto mechanics teacher since, whatever the students may want, you can't find a Latin teacher nowadays. At the same time, there are fewer and fewer students enrolling in foreign language courses even in those colleges that are *not* teacher academies, and there, too, faculties will shrink. One of the first to go — and you can believe that the pygmies will be damn glad to get rid of *him* — will be the the only surviving professor of Attic Greek, a notoriously unreconstructed elitist. He will be replaced by a woman with a right-sounding surname who will teach remedial English as a second language, and she, just as soon as the doddering professor of Old English packs it in, will be joined by another of the same, and a new department will be born.

While all of that has been happening, foreign language study has been continually a victim of propaganda. Because it is not reducible to appreciation, and especially because it requires such antihumanistic behavior as memorization, it has become widely known as a "hard" subject, which is furthermore tainted with elitism. As a result, high school graduates who go to college are less and less likely to choose any course of study in which they will be required to study a foreign language. Where such requirements were once common in anything from English to political science, they must be abolished, lest enrollments shrink, which is the worst thing that can happen in any department. This leads, of course, to further shrinking in the already embattled language department, but what can we do? Surely it is better for the few to suffer than the many. But it also leads to one more abandonment of an intellectual standard and one more submission to the life-adjustment ideology of *Cardinal Principles*, and — after all, those now forgotten language requirements have to be replaced — to one more lie about student outcomes and behavioral objectives for a course in the appreciation of foreign-language-speaking cultures. And, when we have finally reached something like our present condition, when the bad name of language study has provided that few college graduates can even speak English, never mind German or French, and when businesses find that their memo writers can't understand each other, and when thousands of workers are driven out of jobs by foreign competition, then we discover that every Japanese salesman speaks fluent English, and we wonder if that means something.

To whatever other woes it may bring us, of which diminished ability to compete in international trade is only one, we must add another step in the general decline of the intellectual enterprise as a whole, which ought to be the principal business of the schools. This decline, which we can see in science and technology just as well as in the study of the humanities and languages, must continue as long as the inheritors of *Cardinal Principles* continue in all the committees and administrative posts and in all the centers, both

public and private, of educationistic "research." Even when
they are unaware of it, as indeed they often are, all their
notions and theories and programs have an underlying
theme, the theme that is sounded when the ineffective and
thus discontented social studies teacher decides that he would
rather go to those evening classes in educationism and become, instead of a mere teacher, a curriculum facilitator or
a guidance counselor or even, oh joy, an assistant principal.
That theme is compounded partly of a distaste for the work
of the intellect, which he has never been able to do with
pleasure, and partly of the desire to take some revenge on
those who do seem to find that pleasure and in whose eyes
he is a second-class citizen. And the whole apparatus of
theory and governance established in the shadow of *Cardinal
Principles* and now in complete control of public education
in America makes it not only possible but even easy for the
failed social studies teacher to rise above his more intellectual
colleagues and tell them what and how to teach or, even
better, find a place in the eternal task force where needs are
assessed within the parameters of planning whether to plan.
The sought-after jobs in education are the ones that take you
as far as possible from the classroom.

That, by itself, would be splendid, for it would take the
silliest people in the education business away from the places
where they can do the most harm. Unfortunately, however,
all the follies they commit in offices and meeting rooms and
administration buildings and tax-supported agencies are
visited not on their own heads — they pay each other to
think up new follies — but on the heads of the students and
teachers whom they have gladly left behind. Thus it is that,
after about sixty years of organized and militant anti-
intellectualism in the schools, every disorder in education

brings power and profit to those who have made that disorder, and every problem is given for solution into the hands
of the only people who cannot possibly solve it. The pygmies
have been in charge for so long now that we are all cracking
our skulls on the doorways of the public buildings; when
we go to them for remedy, they urge on us the value of
crawling.

Problem-Solving
in the Content Area

W hen we find ourselves wondering about the meaning
of conditions and events, it is always useful to ask,
who profits? The problems and disorders in education have
become more and more visible in the last few years, of
course, and even the ordinary citizen who happens to have
no children in the schools suspects that something is very
wrong, but he will never understand exactly *what* is wrong
until he realizes that all our educational problems and disorders, none of which are new, although they *are* more obvious, provide endless and growing employment for the people
who made them. Barely literate children may be suffering
and facing whole lives of deprivation, but consultants and
remediationists and professors of reading education and tax-
supported researchers and the editors and publishers of work-
books and handsome packets of materials are doing very
well indeed and looking for even better days to come. It is
important to note, too, that all those profit-makers have not
suddenly appeared among us like the wandering bands of
looters who can reasonably be expected to show up after the
earthquake. They've been around a long time, diligently

turning the wheel, professing what must be remediated and remediating what has been professed and enlarging in our society the role of what can only be called the educationist-industrial complex. Anything that may seem to us a disorder in education is for them a golden opportunity — indeed, since they live by tax money, they cannot make their profits until we *do* see a disorder in education and thus feel obliged to shell out.

Curiously enough, therefore, it is very much in the interest of the policymakers and theoreticians of public schooling that there *be* problems and failures and that we know about them and also, even more curiously, that *any* kind of social disorder at all be made the business of the schools. We are encouraged thus to hand over to the educationists not only the problem of widespread illiteracy but also the notorious disinclination of the American voter to trouble himself by going to the polls, the fear and hatred of each race for the others, and the epidemic of venereal disease among thirteen-year-olds.

Sometimes, especially when defending themselves against the charge that they just don't know how to teach reading and writing and ciphering, the educationists complain that they are unfairly burdened by "public demand" for all sorts of social but nonacademic services and instruction. But, in fact, as any reader of *Cardinal Principles* would know, they chose long ago to be social engineers rather than academicians, claiming, too, that they had chosen the nobler calling. It would be interesting to put them to the test, offering them the opportunity to give up all that thankless inculcation of right and worthy feelings and habits and stick to teaching only what can be objectively taught and measured. It would, however, take an enlightened and thoughtful public to make that offer, and the influence of *Cardinal Principles* makes an enlightened and thoughtful public impossible. For all their occasional whimpers, therefore, the educationists are delighted to take upon themselves the right ordering of society, which is, in any case, even more profitable than the cycle of professing and remediating general public illiteracy.

Now here is an interesting and suggestive fact: The seven cardinal principles can be divided, and were in fact divided by their propounders, into two categories. In one category, the category that the educationists themselves have come to call the "cognitive domain," we can put only one principle, the Command of Fundamental Processes, or Basic Minimum Competence. You will recall that once the principle-makers had named the Command of Fundamental Processes they could think of little more to say about it. There is a fascinating truth hidden in that fact: Educationistic research flourishes where it is possible to say a lot about what is vague and withers where there is little or nothing to say about the concrete. About right emotional response to literature you can natter forever, about adding numbers to each other, what else is there to do but teach it? It is partly for that reason, of course, that all the other six principles are in what they now call the "affective domain," where there is no limit to talk. Even vocational education, which you might think would be very concrete indeed, is to be a vehicle for various worthy responses, "right relationships toward fellow workers and society," and even that "clear conception of right relations" between employer and employee, the sort of thing thought useful in East Germany, too. And it is perfectly clear, from *Cardinal Principles* itself and from educationistic theory and practice thereafter, that educationists are much more interested in the six other principles than in the Com-

mand of Fundamental Processes. This is so not only because
the Six can generate more verbiage than the One, but because
the consequences of schooling in the One are embarrassingly
measurable, while the consequences of schooling in the Six
are not only impossible to measure but usually not even dis-
cernible for so many years that, when they do begin to appear, the people who caused them will all be dead, or at least
retired. Thus it is that our educationists are far readier to
offer solutions to disorders in their affective domain than in
their cognitive.

Consider, as a trendy example, sex. In a sane civilization,
to be sure, the citizens would tell the school people that the
sexual attitudes and values of the young were none of the
school's damn business and that they ought to stick to facts,
but we don't do it that way. Our schools have been granted
the sex concession by virtue of those cardinal principles that
put them in charge of Health, in one context, and Worthy
Home-membership, in another. And then there is also the
Worthy Use of Leisure. Thus chartered, the educationists
who have long dabbled in what they call sex education have
now, now that unabashed and self-indulgent libertinism has
brought upon us great plagues of divorce, illegitimate births,
venereal diseases, and all the social and economic and personal disorders attendant on such things, come into their
kingdom. Sex education is in bloom in America.

And what form does it take? What form can it *possibly*
take when it is devised by the inheritors of the cardinal
principles and the manipulators of stimulus and response?
We can, for the sake of convenience although not in any
absolute sense, partition the study of sex, and especially human sexuality, into the educationists' own categories, the
cognitive and the affective. In the one category we can put

everything that we can name and know, all that is objectively demonstrable and subject to reasonable hypothesis and prediction. In the other category we will have to put the other things, the feelings, attitudes, values, and responses, worthy or not, that so fascinated the makers of the cardinal principles. Thus, while the latter considerations can be included with the Six, the former must go with the One. The teaching of certain facts about sex and sexuality is *like* the teaching of reading and writing and ciphering. Knowledge about sex is like any other knowledge, publicly available and publicly verifiable and not variable in accordance with attitudes or emotional responses, however worthy. It is what educationists call "subject matter" — often "mere subject matter" — and can easily be learned without the help of any teacher at all. Most of it is in books, to which a good teacher can, of course, provide useful footnotes in the form of newer knowledge, further description, and the devising of analogies by which facts can be seen as functions of one another and from which hypotheses and principles can be formed. The books do exist, and if students had the habit of reading books there would be no shortage of knowledge about sex. But, because of decades of neglect of the mere subject matter of those fundamental processes, they do not have the habit of reading books any more than the schools have the habit of using books as the primary medium of what is called an education.

The books used in the public schools are almost exclusively books designed specifically to be used in the public schools. This is in keeping with the mandate of *Cardinal Principles* that every course is "in need of extensive reorganization in order that it may contribute more effectively to the objectives outlined herein." A history written by a historian is therefore disqualified unless, by some extraordinary coincidence, it happens to foster the approved responses and appreciations, and that without dependence on mere information. Even should that be so, the book probably would have to be rewritten and simplified for students in whom the Command of Fundamental Processes is meager. A scientist's book on biology, furthermore, would find no place in the schools because it will not be "properly focused upon personal and community hygiene [and] the principles of sanitation, and their applications." To find a welcome in the schools, a book must be simply written — "childishly" might be the better word — and carefully designed to elicit worthy responses, in which cause mere information can be not only dismissed but even distorted. Because it must meet those standards, a schoolbook can never be a mere *book*, as we ordinarily understand the term, a record of the controlled and thoughtful discourse of a knowledgeable, individual mind. To guard against every possible occasion of unworthy response and to root out every appearance of mere information displayed in no cause other than that of mere knowledge requires the diligent labor of a committee in collusion with right-minded consultants and editorial assistants.

In *America Revised* (Atlantic–Little, Brown, 1979) by Frances FitzGerald, you will find a full and demoralizing description of how school history books come to be the perversions that they are. And more recently there was a little-noticed but illuminating example of the nature of school "learning materials" in a Hilton Kramer essay in *The New York Times* on the aftermath of the great Picasso retrospective. The schools are just as good at teaching the right appreciation of art as they are at teaching worthy sexual attitudes, and the Picasso show brought forth not only an "educational" film in which the painter was portrayed, surely to the stupefaction of those with some mere information, as an exemplary parent and role model, but also a teachers' guide in which Picasso is identified as a Fauve playing with bright colors. That's bad enough, but his imaginary enlistment in fauvism is also said to have been a result of his abandonment of experimentation with bright colors. And the cover of the teachers' guide bore a large "Picasso" signature superimposed on a lovely photograph of a studio littered with painter's paraphernalia and handsome canvases, certainly appreciable, but, to anyone having a little knowledge, easily identifiable as the work of Miró.

As bad as this ludicrous display of ignorance is, there is something worse, which Hilton Kramer probably doesn't suspect any more than you do, and that is that no one in the schools is likely to be troubled or embarrassed by such a display. Well, so what? Looking at Miró's studio is *also* a worthy use of leisure, and a niggling attention to trivial details is exactly the kind of elitism that has always inhibited right emotional response. So there. It is in the same spirit that educationists can blithely justify the omission, in an American history text, of any reference to the Civil War.

The making of a schoolbook is analogous to the classroom rap session in which the ill-informed are supposed to reach understanding through the recitation of slogans and notions and by relating to one another. There are differences, however. For the captive children pretending to formulate "good judgment as to means and methods" for the promotion of some worthy social end and developing "habits of cordial cooperation in social undertakings," as prescribed in *Cardinal Principles*, the whole thing is obviously a game. Only a teacher, or an especially dull or cowed student, could take it seriously. But the committees and task forces that devise (you cannot say "write") those non-books used in the schools take their work very seriously indeed. There is profit in it. Even prestige. So we can be confident that the "books," and all the other wondrously diverse and cunningly packaged "learning materials" out of which sex education will be taught, will be acceptable to the ideology of educationism, both simplified and tendentious, careless of mere information and careful in the elicitation of right response in the cause of social adjustment. In other words, this "new" campaign intended to remedy whole hosts of social and personal disorders is different from the old program of education as social manipulation only in extent — and, of course, expense. In both cases, much greater.

As our schools now embark on a massive campaign of sexual rehabilitation for all of American youth, we can naturally expect that they will give it all they have, which means, of course, that what they *don't* have they won't give it. What they do have, *all* they have, is that earnest devotion to the power of suggestion in the cause of social and psychological manipulation, and, although their decades of devotion to pious social adjustment may not be the *only* cause of our present disorders, they have certainly not prevented them. Now the necessary concomitant of the social adjustment theory of education is the denigration of intellectual discipline, for the sake of which the command of fundamental processes was slighted in *Cardinal Principles*. Perhaps it *is* a bit rash, however tempting, to say it is exactly *because* the schools have been preaching vapid and sentimental sermons for sixty years that hosts of our newborn children and their mothers will become permanent wards of the state, but it is not a bit rash to suspect that widespread and crippling social disorders of all kinds are directly caused by ignorance and thoughtlessness. There is only one remedy for ignorance and thoughtlessness, and that is literacy. Millions and millions of American children would today stand in no need of sex education, or consumer education or intercultural education, or any of those fake educations, if they had had in the first place *an* education.

We have seen above, for instance, that what is called intercultural education is a shabby dodge by which students and teachers may be excused from the study of history, anthropology, geography, language, literature, philosophy, and who can count what else. That all makes for a long and detailed discussion, but an equivalent and simpler model of the genesis of fake educations can be seen in the trendy and popular consumer education. We are told that we need consumer education because people are easily duped by misleading advertising, cannot figure out the per-ounce price of ketchup, and imagine that they can live on Twinkies and Coca-Cola. (When teen-aged mothers raise their illegitimate children on Twinkies and Coca-Cola, that reinforces the need for sex education and also family living education.) The consumer who is duped by misleading advertising does not need consumer education; he needs to know how to read. The housewife who can't figure out what ketchup costs does not need consumer education; she needs to know how to cipher. And as to those who want to live on Twinkies and Coca-Cola, frankly that's their own damn business and we ought to leave them alone, but we might legitimately provide them with knowledge about biology and chemistry first and *then* leave them alone. Our problems come not from ignorance and thoughtlessness about sex any more than from ignorance and thoughtlessness about ketchup, they just come from ignorance and thoughtlessness, which are preserved and nourished in our schools by those whose profits lie in "solving" the problems they have created.

Literacy is like the kingdom of Heaven. Those who seek it first will find that other things are added unto them. Literacy is *not* the same as Basic Minimum Competence, but, if we provide an emphasis that seems not to have occurred to the principle-makers, it might indeed be described as the *command* of the fundamental processes of word and number. The power of number, to be sure, is not usually included in "literacy," but it should be, for it is through the ability to *command* the techniques both of word and number that we can know and think. There is no other way. To say that we can "know" or "think" in other ways is to blur those words into uselessness so that rather than making fine distinctions they can point vaguely in the direction of any events at all that seem to take place invisibly in the mind. It is exactly that reluctance to seek or even tolerate fine distinctions that makes the muddled jargon of the educationists what it is, and it is not surprising, therefore, that those who have neglected literacy should look for some presumed *other* ways of knowing and thinking. This makes it possible to excuse or even to justify the failure to teach literacy by claiming that it doesn't have to be taught anyway. Consider the following, a brief and unfortunately oversimplified piece from *The Underground Grammarian*:

The Idea of Expressing
Feelings in New Mexico

It had to happen. Last month we granted the world's first DEd, *horroris causa,* and now everybody wants one. Two new candi-

dates present themselves, and they are not some silly educationists but *bona fide* associate professors of English out at what they
call Eastern New Mexico University.

Laid-back folk. Arlene Zekowski, Stanley Berne. Hate apos-
trophes. Rules. Arbitrary. Down sentences! Up feelings expressing! Up Zekowski! Up Berne! Right on!

Or, if you prefer, On right! "We're professors of English," says
Berne. (Hm. Shouldn't that be "Were professors of English"?)
"We are concerned with the idea of expressing feelings. Arbitrary
rules of grammar prohibit that." (Cmon, be patient. Sure he talks
that tired old grammar, but only because he has to get to we
elitists.) Hes wright. No, thats not expressing feelings. He rite!
Wordsworth feeling-expressing fouled-up by verb-subject agree-
ment. Shakespeare shot down — Donne undone by nonrestrictive
clauses. Whitman comatose from commas.

Zekowski: "Grammar is elitism. I wish to destroy what is
dead, lifeless and snobbish." Hows that for boring from within?
"Arbitrary sentence structure is logical," she complains, "but the
brain isn't logical. [How true!] You don't think in sentences.
You think in terms of patterns and images. It's random association." And further: "Many advertisements don't use sentences or
grammar. They use words to create images." (Exactly *how* they
use the words she docsn't say. Could be they sprinklem here and
there, collage-wise. Cool. Just think. If *Das Kapital* had been
done like that, we wouldn't have all this damn trouble now.
There's nothing more dangerous than a bunch of logical sentences, but what would you expect from an elitist like Marx?)

If there's one thing we love around here, it's the clasting of
icons, and we support the idea of expressing feelings 1,000 percent. That's *exactly* what we should be teaching these kids. For
one thing, it's a cinch, like playing tennis with the net down, as
Frost put it. Another: if we let them in on the secrets of logical
sentences and coherent discourse, the ignorant little bastards will
go on to take away some of our cushiest jobs, perhaps even as

associate professors of English, and that will be the end of lifeless elitism as we know it.

However, while we applaud Zekowski and Berne for their cunning subterfuge, and while we admit that it *is* the first duty of a DEd to cook up schemes for job security, we cannot give them their degrees just yet. Their plan sounds good off paper, but when they write their grammarless English, we read: "Once upon a time ago. But now nevermore." Cute and expressive of feeling, sure, but clogged up with grammar. Maybe next year.

 ——————————————————————————

Following the appearance of that article, I heard from many readers who accused me of inventing Berne and Zekowski. How silly. Bernes and Zekowskis are generated spontaneously out of the primordial nutrient broth of *Cardinal Principles*. If you find them unbelievable, you might be sobered to know that they have written many books for the guidance of public school English teachers and are said to go about holding workshops and training sessions for same.

The "thought" of Berne and Zekowski — I know that's not the right word, but we may not even *have* the right word in English — repays study. Consider: "You don't think in sentences. You think in terms of patterns and images. It's random association." All of that is true, of course, if you happen to be an imbecile, or maybe a gnu. All of it is also true even for conscious human beings *if* the verb *to think* refers to anything, anything at all, that takes place invisibly in the mind. The mind docs indeed, from time to time and often with dismal consequences when there is a certain kind of work to be done, find itself occupied with patterns and images and random associations. And it does many things that have no need of sentences: it regrets, it exults, it yearns, it wonders, it fears, it expects, it dreams (perchance to sleep), it wanders, it sees, it hears . . . you can make your own list. The very fact that there are so many words for the invisible acts of the mind reveals that our language can and regularly does make, as Berne and Zekowski do not, countless fine and subtle distinctions among those acts. And the act in which we *do*, if we have a command of fundamental processes, make such distinctions may be called thinking; and, in fact, we do that thinking in sentences, in which we say to ourselves that yearning and thinking are different for such and such reasons. We may perform any number of mental acts "in terms of," whatever that means, patterns and images, but thinking is not one of them. Thinking is done in sentences, logical sentences. *Principia mathematica* is not random association. Nor, for that matter, is poetry, which Berne and Zekowski are said to write, and which they seem to confuse with "expressing feelings," which could also include smashing urinals in the boys' room. It is one of the great wonders of poetry that it can be supremely free and individual *in spite of* countless traditional and arbitrary restraints, and even in spite of the often greater restraints that poets usually choose to impose on themselves.

Berne and Zekowski, I admit, are probably an extreme case of educationistic anti-intellectualism, but they are, don't forget, professors of English at a state university where English teachers are trained. Their notions are right at home in the context of *Cardinal Principles*. They are concerned with expressing feeling, or, as they put it, with the "idea" of expressing feelings. (I don't know what that might mean, but I suspect that it is *not* some fine distinction between "expressing" and "the idea of expressing.") They wish to destroy elitism, which, although dead and lifeless, somehow manages to remain snobbish. They characterize rules as "arbitrary" rules, as though no one had ever put modifiers near what they modify until the rule had been devised, and assert that the arbitrary rules prohibit the expression of feelings, against which assertion some evidence could be adduced. They turn, for example, to the demotic, the advertisements that "use words to create images," as though that were some startling new use of language and especially to be prized because of its commercial quality. They differ from garden-variety educationists only in detail (and perhaps in their taste for the dramatic — notably absent in educationists) but not in principle. They prefer emotional response to knowledge; they equate technical proficiency with elitism; they imagine grammar as a set of rules, mere information, and the stuff of rote learning; and they depend for their lessons on the popular or practical, to which students can presumably "relate."

When we look around America, we notice, of course, what seems to be a general decline in our young people of the powers of observation and discrimination and the habits of accuracy and precision that we might expect in the literate. This is an illusion born of the fact that it is only the young people who are occasionally tested or measured. The same disabilities are to be found in *all* groups, because they have been fostered for so many years now. And those many years of malpractice have fostered the same disabilities within the ranks of the educationists themselves that we can see in the public at large. The now-retired professors of education who learned *their* appreciation of the "command" of fundamental processes in the shadow of *Cardinal Principles* taught it to the professors of education, who taught the same to all the teachers and supervisors and facilitators now in the schools, who in their turn can pass on to their students nothing but more of the same.

It follows, therefore, that the formulation and direction of the currently faddish fervor for those fundamental processes are given into the hands of those who lack the skills of those processes and who have grown up in the climate of opinion out of which Berne and Zekowski have formulated their principles. The enterprise cannot succeed any more than pygmies can grow tall by pulling upward on their ears.

Here is how one state system of teacher academies plans to solve the problem:

 The Missouri Compromise

You will not be astonished to learn that there are some people in Missouri who cannot manage commas, cannot avoid sentence fragments, cannot regularly make verbs agree with subjects and pronouns with antecedents, and cannot help sounding like literal translations from Bulgarian. If you are a regular reader of this journal, you'll also be unastonished to hear that those pitiable illiterates are members of the Missouri Association of Colleges of Teacher Education.

These poor saps have finally noticed that lots of irate citizens "have indicated concern of [yes, *of*] the decreasing standardized test scores of students." They even know that a "sensitivity has become quite manifest in the development in state wide [yes, two words] assessment systems." But they don't seem too worried. They've cleared up the whole mess in a "position statement" called *Assessment of Basic Skills Competencies of Potential Teachers.*

The Missouri educationists have also just discovered, or have at least come to suspect that they might perhaps decide to assume — tentatively, what the rest of us have always known. They put it thus: "Although many factors may intervene the teacher is viewed by many as a critical variable in the teaching-learning process and, therefore, the key to the improvement in the basic skills of students."

"The teacher," they say, "must have a high degree of proficiency in the basic skills. They are expected to transmit to their students through precept and example."

Yeah. And here are some of the precepts and examples through which these Missouri Teacher-training Turkeys transmit:

"The latter ['field experiences'] being principally in student teaching with a major emphasis on institutional planning, execution, and evaluation of subject matter to be presented." And, "Utilizing the assumption that the measuring/ascertaining of the competencies of potential teachers should be done on or about the end of the traditional sophomore year." For the Turkeys, those are sentences. So why should *they* care? It's the taxpayers and children who'll have to serve them.

Those, of course, are just supersaturated, freebooting participles, but this one passes understanding: "If the student does not meet the prescribed standards of basic skills and the student, before they are formally admitted into teacher education and certainly before graduation, should have remediation and re-evaluation." (Wow, these people are tough! *Before* graduation, no less.) Any competent sixth-grade teacher would flunk such rubbish, but the Turkeys aren't worried. As long as they're in charge, there will be damned few competent sixth-grade teachers in Missouri.

"Also," say the Turkeys, "there is a question of the relationship of secondary and co-secondary schools in terms of relationships. The authors [!] of this position paper agreed that such an assessment process can have a significant impact [they never discuss *insignificant* or *mere* impacts] on secondary school curriculum in turning to an assessment instrument to which the public schools might be inclined to reach toward."

Why do the good people of Missouri suffer such humbug without turning to some blunt instrument to which they might be inclined to reach toward? We can tell you why. It's because these ugly crimes against nature are committed in private among consenting Turkeys. How many "authors," do you suppose, conspired to write, rewrite, edit, and finally to *approve* all that gibberish? How many of Missouri's teacher-trainers, would you guess, have read it? Was *not one* of them embarrassed or outraged by this sleazy display of ignorance and ineptitude? And if there *was* one, what do you think he did? He kept his mouth shut. It's better to suffer a momentary discontent than to attract the taxpayers' attention.

So, unhampered by pesky public outcry, people who cannot devise sentences or make sense or even punctuate will get on with the business of providing Missouri with teachers. And they don't want *any* interference, if you please, as they make, well, not "clear," to be sure, but at least "quite manifest," in their ghastly and ungrammatical peroration:

"There is an advantage to each institution in Missouri preparing teachers to have an institutional level responsibility rather than a state wide . . . responsibility for assurance of proficiency of basic skills. Alternate assessment processes allow for diversity of response by each institution. It [?] allows for diversity of response loads [?] by students, it allows for diversity of interpretation of what is basic [*that's* the part they like best] for that institution's student population, and it eliminates conflicts of perogatives [typo?] and rights of faculties of institution to set curriculum in means of assessing a testing or assuring of competencies."

We have some advice for the good people of Missouri. Turn those rascals out. Pension them off for life at full pay, requiring only that they never again set foot on a campus. Don't worry about the cost. In fifty years or so, there won't *be* any cost. As it is, you're planning to pay more and more of them for ever and ever. Once they're gone, on the day they go, in fact, your schools and colleges will become the best in the land.

A knowledge of history is one of the basic skills of which we have been deprived by the educationists' fervor for shabby social studies and smug civics. We have forgotten that the storekeepers used to pay miscreants to stay *away*. It worked. We've gotten it backward. We pay them to hang around and smash the windows. Let's be realistic and pay the miscreants to do that one thing that we most need them to do — nothing, nothing at all.

I am very sorry to have to award any points at all to the compromisers of Missouri, who are contentedly unconscious of their own ignorance and the ludicrous pathos of their determination to ensure the "measuring/ascertaining" of that "high degree of proficiency in the basic skills," but they do deserve a few. In the first place, if this *is* an exculpation, their ignorance was visited upon them by the system in whose service they labor, and, in the next place, there is much justice in the educationists' routine disclaimer of responsibility for the literacy of incipient teachers. That, they happily point out, is supposed to be the business of the English departments. And they are right, although, if literacy is a fundamental process, it ought to be a concern in *every* department. But there is no doubt that English departments must be charged with teaching everything that can be taught about the technical skills that provide a command of literacy. And Berne and Zekowski, you will surely remember, are professors not of education but of English, who ply their trade in a school where teacher-training happens. Although it is, to be sure, the very existence of the articles of educationistic faith that makes Bernes and Zekowskis *possible*, professors of English are supposed to have some of their *own* articles of faith, which ought to double them up with hysterical laughter when Bernes and Zekowskis appear at department meetings. So the poor professors of education are put in the sad position of having to lament aloud that even the professors of English have swallowed the potion bottled by the professors of education. There's a satisfying sort of justice in that, but it still means that there is not much hope of breaking the cycle in which illiteracy is passed on from generation to generation.

The story of what has happened to English departments in the last few decades, especially in English departments attached to teacher-training academies, would make a fat and dull book. In brief, that history can be seen as a conditioned response to the dual role of the study of English as imagined in *Cardinal Principles*, where the command of fundamental processes on the one hand and the right emotional response to literature on the other were obviously assigned to the same people. Since a fervid dedication to the former has not exactly been a hallmark of the schools, and since the latter can more or less be "taught" by anyone, the teaching of English has evolved into a curious creature that now looks something like a pair of wings with no bird between them. There is the Right Wing, devoted to the study of literature (pronounced in four syllables and without any trace of a "ch"), which has handed over the much-hated and laborious teaching of composition to graduate assistants and junior department members panting after promotion, who look upon the work as a necessary apprenticeship to be swiftly accomplished so that they might go on to teaching seminars in the early Elizabethan dramatists.

The Left Wing is more complicated, because it is divided into two persuasions or parties, the democrats and the technocrats. The democrats are really true inheritors of *Cardinal Principles*, for they propose literature as a vehicle of social and "interpersonal" understanding and an incentive to the appreciation of the brotherhood of all mankind and the human condition. It is the democrats of the Left Wing who have multiplied the offerings in the catalog by cooking up courses in everything from the Urban Experience to Adolescence in America and Female Problems in an Age of Lowered Expectations. Such courses all have, inevitably, their analogues in the high schools, where the study of literature comes down to mini-courses in ghost, sport, or animal stories adapted from popular magazines.

However, while the democrats hold large tracts in the kingdom of government education, the broadest acres are being deeded to the technocrats of the Left Wing, who have prudently provided for themselves and their progeny by reconstruing reading and writing as "communication." Communication is socially acceptable. Even the desultory deliberations of the uninterested ignorant can be called "communication." And the eighth-grade rap session on free abortions for eighth graders suddenly becomes a *skill* to be taught as a legitimate "fundamental process." *All* the presumed skills of communication, including film-making and tape-recorder operation and even (this is true) television-watching, become precincts of the great realm of communications, where writing itself, only one precinct, is subdivided into utilitarian fragments. The study of writing thus gives way to courses in Personal Writing, Creative Writing, Journalistic Writing, Technical Writing — well, however long the list, it will be longer tomorrow.

The innumerable offerings of the communicationists — they sometimes call themselves "communicologists" — recommend themselves in the world of educationism by virtue not only of their collectivist aims but also because of their technical flavor. Idle chatter finds respectability and curricular justification when it becomes Interpersonal Group Communication Methodology. Furthermore, while a course in writing needs only some paper and pencils, courses in communicology can generate some very impressive budgets.

Here is a case in point, indeed, a case in *several* points, for whose sake I must provide some background. The Communications Department in question does its business at the college where I do mine, and it is famous here for having announced its withdrawal from the division of arts and sciences, as we call them. The announcement, a portion of which is quoted, was neither preceded nor accompanied nor followed by any *action* at all. That in itself was a splendid display of the paramountcy of communication over substance. Now, however, there *is* some substance at issue, specifically, a proposal to establish what was then called a "Flagship" program of great excellence in the "field" of communications. (The word "Flagship" cannot be printed out in full in *The Underground Grammarian*):

When the Communications Department blasted off into the unknown regions of interdivisional space, its chairman left us to mull over his now famous Farewell (*sans* Hail):

> But in the sober light of day after the intoxicating elixirs of self-delusion have begun to fade, after the sonorous tones of your voices have begun to sound hollow, after the technicolor hues of your dreams have begun to mute into the blacks and whites of reality — then you may perhaps face these details of reality.

He was reminding us that we had not yet entered the twentieth century, so he must have chosen that quaint and antiquated tone of purple fustian for ironic emphasis — don't you think? How subtly he reminds us of our enslavement to outworn tradition by his innovative use of "mute" as an intransitive verb and that multimedia metaphor in which our elixirs "fade" before our very eyes!

Now the Communications Department re-enters our atmosphere, blazing like another Kohoutek, and bringing no faded elixirs but a heady draft proposal for a F———— of its very own.

We looked at the part where they tell all about the teaching of writing, twentieth-century style. Here's the plan:

> The Communications Department proposes to establish an ideal classroom for the teaching of the basic writing course. . . . While there is no single classroom prototype that could be considered ideal for all circumstances, there is a concern that different approaches be taken. One of the keys in suggesting an ideal classroom is that traditional classrooms have a way of perpetuating traditional approaches. . . . By bringing together in one room a large variety of audiovisual implements, creating a relaxed atmosphere by having the room carpeted with pictures on the walls and easy chairs and tables and by having duplicating equipment and a variety of newspapers and magazines readily available, we can encourage attempts to change both students' perceptions and teachers' approaches to the task of learning how to write.

Now why couldn't we have thought of all that neat stuff? Because we've been hung up perpetuating traditional approaches — things like drill and practice, writing and rewriting — that's why. Even desks! Now we see. What we need is a dentist's waiting room redone by Radio Shack, magazines and Muzak, comfy chairs, and a shiny new Xerox so the scholars won't have to fight over the latest number of *Popular Mechanics*.

Notice a refreshing absence of flat, empty surfaces where a thoughtless student might accidentally write words on a piece of paper and set the whole class back a century. That's the hard part, all right, putting the words on the paper. That's why hardly anyone was able to write before the advent of that large variety of audiovisual implements. (*Implements?*)

The proposal itself seems to have been put together in just such an innovative, relaxing setting. Notice, for instance, the creative (or easy chair) treatment of punctuation in that bit about the pictures. The room is carpeted with pictures on the walls. The pictures are on the walls and easy chairs and tables. It's a split-screen effect. Elec*tron*ic!

Elsewhere we find:

> A second prong in the outreach of the department would come from a Communication Consultancy Center. This would be created as an umbrella from which many different kinds of services could be offered to the community.

Stunning. No fuddy-duddy of the age of paper and pencil could ever have accomplished prose like that. The secret is "vision." Only a writer who has learned his craft from long hours of assiduous (but relaxed) scrutiny of a twenty-inch color implement could hope to develop a vision modern enough to see that outreaches have prongs, prongs coming from their Centers, and that a prong, or maybe a Center, can be created as an umbrella, an umbrella from which services can be dispensed, services that can help us all to learn how to communicate in just this fashion.

Well, you can just bet your Bearcat scanner against a busted quill pen that all our staff writers will be standing at the door the day they open that Communications Consultancy Center. We're mired in traditions. We could never, for instance, have come up with these spiffy structures that go the tired old passive at least one better — maybe two:

> . . . [the] Department can provide leadership that will cause it to be viewed as a resource . . .
> . . . few of the courses . . . have been able to be offered on a regular basis.
> . . . needs should be able to be filled . . .

You just can't hope to master that smooth modern style without spending hours, whole *seasons* probably, in the old easy chair, beer and pretzels at hand, studying the styles of the greatest play-by-play and color men to be found on the audiovisual implement.

And just look at these daring departures from stodgy tradition. We're so old-fashioned that we almost thought they were mistakes:

> . . . the advantages the computer offers . . . lies in its continuous availability.
> . . . the equipment needs . . . is appended.
> . . . there needs to be provisions made . . .

All of this is encouraging for anybody who worries about the teaching of writing here at Glassboro. It shows that the Communications Department is perfectly willing to put some of the taxpayers' money where somebody's mouth is — in a collection of machines. Time was when your basic model communications teacher would rather watch reruns of "Washington Week in Review" than teach a writing course. Now they'll be clamoring to twiddle the dials and leaf through *Cosmopolitan* and rap about nontraditional approaches to interpersonal communication in the easy chair.

So not to worry. We can all go down to the launching in good conscience, sing in our hollow tones one chorus of "Anchors Aweigh," smash a fifth of faded elixir on the prow of the refitted Starship Triad, newly home from one uncharted deep, sallying forth into yet another, carrying our hopes and dreams, ere they mute, our tuners and amplifiers and, of course, the prongs of our outreach.

 ❖ —————————————————————————— ❖

In that blazing display of furniture and equipment, you may have missed the fact that the "ideal classroom" (certainly ideal for some lucky contractors) is for "the teaching of the *basic* writing course." Advanced courses in various "writings" will require yet more specialized doodads. The implicit suggestion of all the paraphernalia and even the carefully designed environment will be the same, to wit, that writing is just one of many "skills" of communication, similar *in kind* to the making of television commercials and the grammarless collages that so pleased Berne and Zewokski. And it follows that "reading" is the skill of receiving and registering "communication," which, accordingly, may or may *not* come in the form of writing. And it further follows, therefore, that what the schools mean by "literacy" is not what you think it is. Literacy may be "visual literacy" or the ability to program computers, although it is hard to imagine how people who are not interested in punctuation or spelling can meet the even more stringent demands of computer programs.

But the greatest achievement of the communicationists, and the one that best assures their prosperity, is that they have transformed writing from a private act into a public one, from a solitary search for understanding into a public display of some communication. This suggests some deeper reasons, deeper than their obvious distaste for the mere information required in the teaching of writing, for the *pro forma* mention and subsequent neglect of those fundamental processes in *Cardinal Principles*. Everywhere in that pamphlet, we can find exhortations to socialization through group efforts, group discussions, group thinking, and even games and dances. We find specific condemnations of too much knowledge of mere facts and too much attention to intellectual discipline, characteristic foreshadowings of that later indictment of "excellence narrowly defined." In an even more recent policy statement from the National Education Association, *Curriculum Change Toward the 21st Century* (1977), a reappraisal and expanded reaffirmation of *Cardinal Principles*, we read:

> Imbedded in the question of freedom is an educational dilemma — the long-standing enigma of how to obtain the important output of superior minds without creating an elite of scientists, politicians, social planners and commentators, military specialists, business executives, and so on.

Or, in other words, how can we manage to muzzle the ox while he treadeth out the corn?

The supposed love of democracy out of which the commissioners devised their principles is really just a hatred of those "superior minds," from which, notice, we can profit *not* by the study and practice of superior mindfulness but by "obtaining their output." While we will discourage students from a painful retracing of the path of Newton's logic, for instance, we will take profit and pleasure from the fact that Newton has made it possible (for some *few* of us, who do have to be watched carefully for signs of incipient elitism) to construct devices that work.

But we mustn't forget that bullet, the one that "spins" end over end in perfect but antisocial obedience to the laws of motion. (A thoughtful writer would have written "tumbles," but, having done that out of thoughtfulness, he would probably, out of that same thoughtfulness, have understood that the point of the example was utterly irrelevant.) Of the output that we might obtain from those superior minds, some must prove unworthy, which is to say, antihumanistic, which in turn is to say, the work of an individual mind heedless of collective values. It is thus a primary aim of social adjustment educationism to disarm and overwhelm the individual mind and replace it with a comprehensive data bank of received and unexamined attitudes, values, opinions, and worthy emotional responses. All of the curricular dilutions and manipulations prescribed in *Cardinal Principles* are means to that end. And, to that end, there is only one certain impediment. It is the one "student outcome" that our schools simply cannot afford to provide, even if they could, which, out of thoughtless acceptance of their own principles, they can't. It is, of course, literacy.

"Literacy" needs some redefining. When Jefferson spoke of that literacy that would provide "informed discretion," he did not mean the ability to read the instructions for assembling a swing set or even for assembling a nuclear power generating plant. He did not mean the ability to write a correctly punctuated letter of application for a job. He did not mean the ability to devise, or even to "appreciate," advertisements that "use words to create images." He did not mean the habit of worthy emotional response to literature. In short, he did not mean any, or even all taken together, of those "skills" that we now put forth as studies in communications or language arts. He did mean certain habits and powers of the individual mind, habits and powers that can be learned and refined only by long practice in reading and writing.

Literacy is not, as it is considered in our schools, a *portion* of education. It *is* education. It is at once the ability *and* the inclination of the mind to find knowledge, to pursue understanding, and, out of knowledge and understanding, not out of received attitudes and values or emotional responses, however "worthy," to make judgments. Literate people are *not* easy prey. They do know an inference from a statement of fact. They are not easily persuaded by pretended authority. They are attentive to the natural requirements of logic. They can make distinctions, very fine distinctions, and are able both to notice and to examine their own predispositions and even their only presumably "right emotional responses." To say that young human beings are incapable of such powers *is* elitism.

But our schools do say that. And thus they not only preclude those powers in the students but in the whole system. Today's teachers and the teachers of today's teachers are all the inevitable results of the system. They simply don't know what literacy is. This accounts for one of the most bewildering contradictions to be found in the current pandemonium of bold, innovative thrusts in basic minimum competencies. On the one hand, our educationists fancy that literacy is something you achieve when you have developed enough "skills." But it turns out that many of those skills are in fact the results of much practice and hard knowledge and habits of rote learning and mere information, things in short supply not only among the hapless students but also among the teachers and the teachers of the teachers. Therefore, on some other hand, having discovered how hard it is to teach those skills in a system where *no one* is very good at them, the educationists can also fancy that literacy is *not* simply a matter of skills, which now become "mere" skills, and that it might just as well be achieved in their absence.

"Problem-solving in the content area" is a favorite pastime of educationists. In the case of literacy, it works this way: Literacy, *whatever* it is, must be a student outcome. So let's try to teach those basic skills and offer mini-courses and interesting electives in all sorts of communications and language arts and let the students express themselves and improve their self-esteem. Then we'll find out what the student outcomes are and call them "literacy." Put in those terms, the proposition sounds too preposterous to win approval even among educationists, unless you happen to be one of millions of American parents who have wondered how compositions full of uncorrected and perhaps unnoticed mechanical errors could earn such good grades.

The convenient redefinition of literacy, however, is not merely a happy dodge for teachers. It is national policy in the realm of educationism, which embraces even those outlying provinces that we mistakenly deem buffer states between us and the traditional expansionism of governmental social adjustment. The same comfortable and undemanding re-definition is a matter of policy at the Educational Testing Service:

 The Holistic Hustle

Fortunately for American educationists, there is never any dearth of trashy and popular fads, the raw material of curricular novelty. The half-life of most bold innovative thrusts is less than that of the pet rock or the nude encounter group, and pedagogical gimmicks have to be cooked up more often than situation comedies. But, thanks to the fertile inventiveness always inspired by exuberant greed, the master schlockmongers will always provide the educationists with full measures of readily adaptable inanities.

Of course, there is a difference between the peddlers of pop and the educationists. The peddlers of pop are skillful. When promoters have deposited the take from Woodstocks and Earth Days, the educationists come limping behind with mini-courses in the "poetry" of rock and roll, and environmental awareness. In a frantic scramble after what crumbs may fall from the merchants' tables, they rush to "teach" soap-opera-watching, the casting of horoscopes, and the throwing of the Frisbee. Coming soon: Elvis, the copper bracelet, and the T-shirt as literature.

Future historians of education (how's that for a dreary calling?) will understand better than we that the most powerful influence on education in our time was not new knowledge of the psychology of learning, not the rise and dominance of the electronic media, not the fervor for democratization that followed the civil rights movements, not even the newly awakened public recognition of the tensions between the demands of an increasingly automated society and a reinvigorated and often anti-materialistic individualism, but, purely and simply, the Big Mac. Our schools are, in almost every respect, analogues of the fast-food industry, although there probably is some nourishment in the Big Mac. Even the slogans are the same: Have it *your* way; We do it all for yoo-oo-oo.

It's not surprising, therefore, that educationists respond to public discontent not by trying to improve what they do, but by trying to "educate" the public into some other "perception" of what they do. In education, as in the fast-food business, it's called "image enhancement," and, like all flackery, it's done with slogans and buzz words. When the public finally noticed, for instance, that fewer and fewer children were learning to read, the educationists quickly discovered that "learning disabilities" were far more common than anyone had ever suspected. Therefore, we ought in fact to *praise* the schools for doing such a great job with swarms of undernourished, disaffected imbeciles, many of whom were also myopic, hard of hearing, hyperactive (if not lethargic), or even lacking in self esteem.

Now, pestered by complaints about student writing, the educationists have drawn from the bottomless pit of mindless pop a bucket of inspiration, the Whatever Turns You On Plan for the Enhancement of Public Perceptions Concerning Student Writing. They call it "holistic" grading. It will improve grades dramatically without requiring any improvement in the teaching of writing. It will work even in schools where there is *no* teaching of writing. Now *that's* educationism.

Most of what we've heard about holistic grading has come from the horse's mouth, the National Council of Teachers of English. We now have a report from another part of the horse, the Educational Testing Service, which is offering "workshops" in holistic grading:

> With this method, the essay is read for a total impression of its quality rather than for such separate aspects of writing skill as organization, punctuation, diction, or spelling. The method takes a positive approach to the rating of compositions by asking the reader to concentrate on what the student has accomplished rather than on what the student has failed to do or has done badly. Holistic scoring is both efficient and accurate. The standards by which compositions are judged are those that the readers have developed from their training and from their experiences with student writing.

We have to presume that the written parts of tests given by ETS will be "rated" in this "efficient and accurate" fashion from now on. In a few years, we'll hear that the writing crisis, if indeed there ever was one, is over.

This, you see, is a "positive approach." To fuss about organization, punctuation, diction, and spelling is the bad old negative approach that caused the whole flap to begin with.

To judge writing by this "holistic" method is like judging a musical performance without reference to rhythm, tempo, or dynamics, and taking no heed of false notes or of "organization." What could we say of a performance in which all of those things were wrong? We could certainly *not* judge it as a musical performance if we choose to give no weight to the attributes of musical performance. If we could consider things without regarding their attributes, which we can't, we wouldn't even know what the hell they were. It is only by their attributes that we can distinguish a musical performance from a billiard ball. It is by just such attributes as organization and diction, dismissed above as presumably optional "aspects," that we can distinguish between written composition and the egg stains on an educationist's face.

And *that* is a distinction that we had better learn to make. There will never be good, universal, public education in America until we learn, from their own words, that the people in charge of it are badly in need of an education. Educated people will not be deceived by such nonsense. Some knowledge of the history of thought and some skill in logical language can be expected of the educated, but they are not required for a degree in "education."

Educated people are likely to know what "holistic" means. They know, simply because they have the power of language and thought, that if something is *more* than the sum of its parts, it cannot be *less* than the sum of its parts. They even know what "aspects" are, and that to call punctuation, spelling, diction, and even organization, "separate aspects" of writing suggests either ignorance or mendacity. They know, too, that this slick hustle, designed not only to deceive the taxpayers about the state of student writing but also to make the grading of compositions one hell of a lot easier, may appropriately be called many things, but "holistic" isn't one of them.

"Contemptuous," however, *is* one of them. It is not out of kindness but out of contempt (and sloth) that educationists design ways to excuse students from the demands of good work. To tell a student that "what he has accomplished," however little that may be, is an adequate substitute for "what he has failed to do or has done badly," however much *that* may be, is not "humanistic" (they don't know the meaning of that word, either) or even humane. It is arrogant.

It is also unmistakably to imply that the mastery of good writing is not important. Do you suppose that those educationists would want their dentists or even their electricians "rated" by their "holistic" method? When pilots and flight engineers are licensed by "positive approaches" without regard for all those trivial "separate aspects" of their crafts, will the loyal members of the National Council of Teachers of English fly to the annual convention *anyway,* just to demonstrate their faith in a "total impression of quality"? Will they consult physicians whose diplomas have been granted in spite of "what the student has failed to do or has done badly"?

One thing must be said in fairness to the educationists who have packaged and touted the Holistic Hot 'n' Juicy: The standards by which they propose to measure students' work are no more rigorous than those by which they judge their own work. After all, the ability to write good English isn't required for a doctorate in education, so why bother high school kids about it? Of course, there may be some kids who aim higher and would like to do useful and respectable work that calls for the habits of accuracy and clear thought that come from the mastery of written composition, but the fast-food business doesn't work that way. When ETS serves up the Holistic Hot 'n' Juicy, everybody eats it.

And the educationists all get to do a little something for themselves too-oo-oo.

 ──

In a school where "holistic rating" is accepted orthodoxy, will a student's understanding of the mere facts of human sexuality be measured, and applauded, out of a total impression of its quality? Will the mindless appreciation of expressed feelings in grammarless (and successful) advertisements have some consequence in the classroom next door where children are learning to be canny consumers? Having completed their courses in sex and consumer education, will students be every bit as knowledgeable and thoughtful in their sex lives and their ketchup selection as they are in the separate aspects of writing skills? Will it come to pass with them in the world according to whatever little they may have "accomplished" rather than according to what they have done badly or failed to do?

In the absence of literacy and the habits of mind that it both induces and permits, no one can understand anything, for understanding is not the same as knowing. What we know can be expressed in statements about the world. What we understand has to be expressed in statements *about* statements about the world. Understanding calls for classification and organization, fine distinctions, and logical testing, all related to knowledge. All of those things *can* be taught in schools to very young children, but they can *not* be taught where an "impression" of overall quality supersedes the measurement of "separate aspects of writing skills," which are precisely the devices of classification and organization, fine distinctions, and logical testing. There is thus an absolute limit imposed on what the schools can do in the zany "educations." Even should the schools be able to provide some knowledge about human sexuality, for instance — and that itself is not to be counted on in an atmosphere hostile to mere information and rote learning — they will never be able to provide understanding until they have first provided literacy.

That absolute limit can also be understood in social and political terms, terms of the educationists' own devising. We have seen that even the technically skillful and ingenious, to say nothing of the educated (not always the same thing), are beheld by the educationists with wary suspicion. They may well be the products of that "excellence narrowly defined" that has fouled the air and water, and they are certainly the incipient elitists who constitute that "dilemma" in the form of a "long-standing enigma." Is there perhaps some danger in a program of sex education that gets too close to "excellence narrowly defined?" Will some lurking "superior minds" seize the opportunity to become more knowledgeable and thoughtful than most of their classmates and become as skillful and effective in matters sexual as they are in designing those demonic transistors? Will they become a sexual elite, leading prudent and orderly lives in stable families, from which privilege the great mass of Americans is unjustly excluded? And from such a privileged elite, which uses its thoughtfulness and knowledge exclusively in its own private interests, how can we obtain any useful output?

Since our educational system thrives on the disorders it causes, such questions are not as farfetched as they may sound. A case in point is the new and much-talked-of "awareness" among educationists of a looming and promising problem that will bring hosts of new programs, research grants, administrators, counselors, facilitators, and specialists: the fact that children who live with only one parent don't, as a group, do as well in school as children from what is coming more and more to be thought of as a special case, an "intact family." That is, at least in part, a problem of sexual values, attitudes, and habits. While the children who live with only one parent may be in some personal distress, their growing numbers are good for business. The workshops alone will provide employment for thousands. On the other hand, any significant diminution in their numbers would be bad for business. It is not realistic to suppose that a massive governmental institution will do anything that will someday give it less to do.

There is, in fact, no "problem-solving in the content area," although there are certainly problems "in the content area." But in a government institution, there is only one area in which problems are taken seriously, and that is the political. Many of the strange things done in American educationism suddenly become perfectly understandable when we see them not as educational methods but as political maneuvers. We must understand illiteracy, therefore, the root of ignorance and thoughtlessness, as not some inadvertent failure to accomplish what was intended but simply a political arrangement of great value to somebody.

Every Three Second

ℰ ducationists are entertaining. We can always find a good laugh in their prose, with its special, ludicrous combination of ignorance and pretentiousness. It's always amusing to watch them reinventing the wheel every few years and announcing, for instance, as some of them recently have, that children who know the sounds of letters can actually read words they've never seen before, by golly. It's fun to consider the systems of Lilliputian leaping and creeping by which they better their lots and advance from humble teaching to exalted posts as curriculum facilitators, and the superintendent's speech at the athletic awards banquet usually has that rarest of literary qualities, absolute immunity to parody. Indeed, the first thing you see when you consider thoughtfully and in some detail the ways of American educationism is that it is funny. It's usually the last thing you see, too, and since education is not one of the truly *serious* enterprises of American civilization, like petrochemicals or banking, it doesn't seem to matter much. True, clowns and kooks seem common in the education business, especially at the higher managerial levels, but so what? The whole business is about nothing more than children, who don't count yet, and who can't be expected to do any important work. We are quite ready to tolerate in curriculum and governance the same clumsy amateurism that we find so engaging in the school play and the marching band. After all, weren't we all taught in our own time in the schools that what *really* counts is the effort? And it is only when we go to the home games that we hope to see excellence.

We tolerate the educational establishment the same way that we tolerate the children themselves, and we therefore extend to the guidance counselors and curriculum facilitators the same immunities that we extend to the children, the harmless children. They are all together — over *there* — aside from the mainstream of *real* life. But anyone who will look long and carefully at what happens "over there" will sooner or later notice something that doesn't seem funny. He may begin to suspect that perhaps there *are* some consequences to child's play, and that maybe the children aren't so harmless after all, to say nothing of the counselors and facilitators. It may begin to dawn on such an observer that the children in school actually *are* people and not merely yet-to-be-formed raw materials who will start to be people after the last blackboard has been washed. Where once he tolerated the silliness of the schools as a temporary and sectarian custom in a small fragment of real life, he now sees that the habits and attitudes so earnestly inculcated in children by silly people will almost certainly *not* evaporate on commencement day. And why should they? Habits and attitudes never evaporate. We may sometimes change them consciously, but only after skillful observation and controlled thoughtfulness, which are generally *not* among the habits and attitudes that children acquire in school. Those are the habits of literacy. The attentive and patient observer, therefore, must come to see at last that school is not "something else over there." School is America. If you want to predict the future of our land, go to school and look around.

Schools do *not* fail. They succeed. Children *always* learn in school. Always and every day. When their rare and tiny compositions are "rated holistically" without regard for separate "aspects" like spelling, punctuation, capitalization, or even organization, they *learn*. They learn that mistakes bring no consequences. They learn that their teachers were only pretending in all those lessons on spelling and punctuation. They learn that there are no rewards for good work, and that they who run the race all win. They learn that *what* they win is a rubber-stamped smiling face, exactly as valuable as what they might lose, which is nothing, nothing at all. They learn that the demands of life are easily satisfied with little labor, if any, and that a show of effort is what really counts. They learn to pay attention to *themselves*, their wishes and fears, their likes and dislikes, their idle whims and temperamental tendencies, all of which, idolized as "values" and personological variables, are far more important than "mere achievement" in subject matter. The "whole child" comes first, and no one learns that lesson better than the children. Just as you can predict the future by going to school, you can decipher the past by looking around. All those thoughtless, unskilled, unproductive, self-indulgent, and eminently dupable Americans — where have they been and what did they learn there?

What is done to children in schools is not inconsequential. It is not even the "fun and games" that might be deplored for its own sake. It is permanent and deadly serious. Sometimes, it is simply deadly:

When you talked us in your paper you called us barbarians. It is even more rude than when you call us delinquents. You cant compare us to 50 years ago because we dont wear knickers' and deliver newspapers. All you Old Farts are the same. At Cominsky Park we were just expressing our feelings about disco, because disco sucks. If you write another column like that you will have to answer to me in person.

> A letter to Mike Royko
> from a high school student

I was struck by a manifest shallowness in the doer [Eichmann] that made it impossible to trace the incontestable evil of his deeds to any deeper level of roots or motives. The deeds were monstrous, but the doer . . . was quite ordinary, commonplace, and neither demonic nor monstrous. There was no sign in him of firm ideological convictions or of specific evil motives, and the only notable characteristic one could detect in his past behavior as well as in his behavior during the trial and throughout the pre-trial police examination was something entirely negative. it was not stupidity but *thoughtlessness*. . . . Is wickedness, however we may define it, this being "determined to prove a villain," *not* a necessary condition for evil-doing? Might the problem of good and evil, our faculty for telling right from wrong, be connected with our faculty of thought?

> Hannah Arendt, in
> *The Life of the Mind*

Mike Royko is a columnist at the *Sun-Times* of Chicago. His essays appear in many newspapers throughout the country, thank goodness, for he has the habit of clear language and thought. Mike Royko wrote a column about those eleven people who were trampled to death at a rock concert in Cincinnati. He suggested, by no means injudiciously, that "those who would climb over broken bodies to reach a seat in an auditorium could be called 'the new barbarians.' " That suggestion must have seemed less than humanistic and perhaps even somewhat un-self-esteem-enhancing to a certain Robert Maszak, a teacher of English at Bloom Township in Chicago Heights. Maszak, probably remembering his training in the teacher academy, seized for his students this marvelous opportunity for a relevant and experiential exercise in the integration of self-awareness aspects and the clarification of values. He had them all write letters telling Royko where to head in, and proving, since they *could* write, that some teenagers were not barbarians. In fact, they couldn't, and they are.

Royko, to be sure, had said nothing about teen-agers — or about the worth of rock music, which was stridently championed in many of the letters. Maszak, however, may well be a member of the National Council of Teachers of English, and thus both a proponent and a practitioner of "holistic" reading, in which the reader must scrupulously refuse to consider what the writer actually says, a mere "aspect" of writing.

Maszak may also be a holistic grader, for he was not reluctant to display the fruits of his teaching, which look like this:

> Dear Tenage hater
> I was disapointed by what you writen on the Who concert. From what you said I can see you have know so called barbarism. You used some strong words in there with very little fact, you say everyone was numbed in the brain. I will say from concert experience maybe half or three forths were high on something or nether but I allso know that theres not one forth to half that weren't. You say everyone was pushing and throwing elbows, did you ever think that some of the thrown elbows were from people who didn't like getting pushed. You said something about when you were a kid, well times have change. . . .

Yes. The times indeed have change. Well, let's try to be holistic. Let's ignore failures of technique and, as we were instructed in last month's quotation from ETS, concentrate on "what the student has accomplished rather than on what the student has failed to do or has done badly." Let's remember as well the aggrieved whimpers of the educationists who beseech us to believe that skill in writing is obviously, while useful, much less important than humanistic things like the encouragement of self-expression, the enhancement of self-esteem, and the clarification of values.

Now we can understand why Maszak was untroubled by such a piece of work. It is, in fact, a testimony to the triumph of educationism over education. That poor student, not a villain but a victim, has indeed expressed nothing more than *himself*. His esteem for that forlorn and meager self is firm and truculent. And his values are perfectly clear.

Perfectly clear, too, are the values of the few students who actually mentioned Royko's topic, the death of eleven people. One saw it as a perfectly expectable concomitant of everybody's inalienable right to have what he wants when he wants it. Here's his clarification of values:

> If there were someone yer looked up to and yer went to see them in person and thier were thousands of peopl just like you and wanted to see him up close would you fight yer way in?

Another shows an even keener sense of values; he gives us the very numbers by which we can reconcile ourselves to death in Cincinnati: "People die every three second. What would you do if you paid $15 for a ticket?"

Eichmann must have said as much in the still watches of the night, if he ever *did* say anything to himself. Jews die anyway, don't they? And Eichmann had even more than fifteen dollars at stake.

You can be sure that the humanisticists in our schools will make a profit from that last letter. They will transform it into a "values clarification module": You have paid for a ticket to hear a concert by the Walking Dead, whom yer look up to. How cheap does it have to be for you to decide that getting to your seat just isn't worth the hassle of trampling a few people to death, people who may in any case die every three second? The ensuing rap session will be quite long enough to provide yet another day's respite from the tedious and dehumanizing study of language and thought.

The children who wrote the Royko papers are juniors and seniors in high school. They are probably from sixteen to nineteen years old. They have spent eleven, twelve, or more, years in our "humanistic," "values-oriented," schools. What their teachers have praised as "creativity" looks remarkably like anarchic self-indulgence, which is what creativity must always be in the want of discipline and skill. Their much-encouraged "self-expression" cannot be distinguished from dissolute libertinism, a virulent form of self-expression where there is no self-knowledge. Their "enhanced self-esteem" has blossomed into an arrogant narcissism, a perversion of self-esteem where there is no idea of what is estimable.

Can we hope that Maszak's few students are unique, or at least unusual? We cannot. We know that there are millions, millions of children who have in effect been *dehumanized* by the "human-istic" education that smugly dismisses the mastery of knowledge and skills and the discipline of the intellect as elitist adornments accessible, if they *will* have them, only to the few, and eagerly peddles to the many the mindless claptrap of environmental awareness and career orientation and ethnic sensitivity and doing your own thing and letting it all hang out.

Human beings only, of all living creatures, can know what Hannah Arendt has described as "the claim on our thinking attention that all events and facts make by virtue of their exis-tence." She said of Eichmann "that he clearly knew of no such claim," although she does not say of him, as we might have to of Maszak's students, that even had he known of such a claim he would have proved incapable of paying it *thinking* attention.

Thinking attention can be paid only in skillful language. And, for those who want to be humanistic, there is no more distinctly human attribute than the power of language and no more distinctly human accomplishment than thinking attention.

Go and learn *those* things, you humanism-mongers, before you presume to instruct our children in values. And do it fast. There isn't much time. We have read the Royko papers, and we know what you have been doing. We have seen the future that you have fashioned for us, and, in words that even your victims will understand, it sucks, humanisticists, and all the *young* farts are the same.

It is possible, of course, to make too much of what seems a smoldering savagery in the students of Robert Maszak. But when we seek mitigation of that ominous threat to the future of an already disintegrating civilization, we discover yet other threats. For instance, it is probably true that Maszak's teen-agers are in part striking poses designed to disturb grown-ups, *pour épater*, no doubt, *le bourgeois*. That is not only a child's inalienable right, but an important part of the training of the mind. Rational thoughtfulness, after all, is not and should not be the ordinary condition of daily human life; it is a stance that we assume, if we can, when appropriate. Even if we are able to do the work of logical thinking, we do not, unless we are John Stuart Mill, perhaps, do it except in response to a summons, exactly the summons that Hannah Arendt has in mind when she speaks of "the claim . . . that all events and facts make by virtue of their existence." Attentive thoughtfulness is an aberration, an act not only rare in human experience but also an act requiring cultivation. Thinking is not unlike playing the violin; it isn't simply natural. Even if we can do it, we don't often do it.

Very well, then. We admit that those teen-agers are, in part at least, striking stances. But why these and only these stances? What stance, we wonder, has their teacher himself chosen, so that they can so obviously expect his approval? Their chosen stance is (just like their teacher's?) tiresomely ordinary and predictable; even its virulent truculence is exactly what "tough" teenagers suppose "stylish." It pretends to express an independence, especially an independence of the outworn values of grown-ups who wore knickers and delivered newspapers, but it in fact expresses the opposite, for it is nothing but a recitation of attitudes and emotions as generally received and accepted in that milieu. "That milieu" includes the classroom, obviously, and the school. It includes principally, however, the world *out there*, the popular, the ideology of the streets and the movies and the music. In that sense, Maszak's classroom *is* the world, only less so, for it repeats what is uttered first in the world. The agents of

American educationism do not *lead* their students anywhere, they *follow* them, and always downstream, always in the way they would go even if there were no schools.

An education, which requires the training of the mind in rational thoughtfulness, goes against the grain. It isn't easy. It isn't even "natural," as we usually mean that word. To live, even to live an ordinary and comfortable life, requires the practice of rational thoughtfulness no more than it requires practice on the violin. You can come and go, get and spend, work and play, choose and reject, rise and fall, live and die, entirely in response to the suggestions without and the appetites within. You need never feel, never mind answer, that claim that facts and events make on the thinking attention. For any value you share, any "worthy" emotional response to which you are led, any received opinion that you think to call "yours," there is always the justification of some fifteen-dollar ticket.

Furthermore, a whole culture composed of people just like you would be a very stable and peaceful one. While the social-adjustment educationists may seem silly and ignorant, at the heart of all they do there is an important and correctly understood truth: thoughtfulness *is* disruptive, and the work of an individual mind is seldom likely to contribute to the consistent harmony of a collective social system. Therefore, while you, as an individual mind, may judge that the children who wrote to Royko suggest some failure in schooling, and while such might even be the judgment of individual minds who actually *do* the schooling, those same children represent a mighty success *in principle*. Whatever else they might be, they are not individual minds that will fall into the anticollective habit of thoughtful attention. They may indeed make a ruckus at a rock concert, which is ironically only a part of the "consistent harmony of a collective social system," but they will not examine and reexamine the ideas and values that have been delivered unto them.

Those students represent another kind of success. Their schools have undertaken, at the expense of skills and knowledge, to instill in them values. And they have values. They know what a fifteen-dollar ticket is worth and that disco sucks. Those *are* values. They are not determinations from evidence, not descriptions of phenomena, not conclusions from argument. They are assertions of worth. Values. They are neither unusual nor eccentric, however repellent some may find them. But even the most intemperate critic of American educationism cannot accuse the schools of *intending* to teach such values, and the people in the schools will themselves protest that such reprehensible values are picked up *not* in the schools, which struggle bravely and perhaps hopelessly against them, but from "the society." They are right, and they are wrong. Certainly the resort to violence, hedonistic self-indulgence, and the supposed worth of whatever is popular are celebrated in "the society." But why is that so? It must be because we are in the habit of accepting values out of suggestion and example rather than of formulating them out of knowledge and thoughtfulness. And *that* must be so because we have been schooled into that habit, for whose sake we have been unschooled in the habit of thoughtful judgment, which would preclude the habit of accepting values out of suggestion and example and make impossible the social adjustment that is the principal aim of the schools. Thoughtful judgment is a specific antibody against uncritical susceptibility to suggestion, so it must be repressed if schooling is to succeed. And when it is repressed successfully, through willful neglect of intellectual discipline and mere information, schoolchildren will form their "values" not from the transparent preachments of teachers who are obviously trying to con them into putting on knickers and delivering newspapers, but from the dramatic and stylish examples of the world of the demotic.

Many pernicious consequences flow from the fact that the schools have appointed themselves inculcators of values and that the American public, itself "adjusted" by the schools, has come to believe that the inculcation of values *is* a legitimate aim of education. One of the worst of those consequences is now made manifest in the current wave of sectarian demands that the schools, since they *are* in the values business anyway, ought to teach not just the nonsense they have been teaching but whatever other nonsense any sufficiently noisy group of citizens may prefer. After all, if the schools can "teach" doing your own thing or going with the flow (*both* of which, curiously enough, can justify any particular belief or deed), why can't they "teach" that the universe is just as well described in Genesis as in geology, astronomy, paleontology, physics, biology, and chemistry? While they preach, from one side of the mouth, a humanistic contempt for that "excellence narrowly defined" that brought us all those ugly antennas, why can't they prate, from the other, about the glories of the profit system? There is no good answer to such questions. If a tax-supported government school system devotes itself to *any values at all*, it can always be made to do exactly that for any *other* values at all.

One of the inevitable consequences of sixty years of anti-intellectualism in the government schools is the automatic assumption of most Americans that things like spelling and punctuation are political and ideological badges. Those who are fussy about spelling and punctuation, and other such devices, are assumed to be old-fashioned, conservative, and elitist, while those who care little for such traditional trivia must be with it, liberal, and democratic. (This accords ill with another article of American folklore, according to which it is the "educated" who become liberals and abandon the old-time religion of this or that, but the American public has been trained not to see such contradictions.) Because *The Underground Grammarian* often ridicules academicians who cannot spell or punctuate or even make sense, readers occasionally assume that it must also be against gun control and in favor of prayer in schools and a return to McGuffey's Readers. I often had letters from strange people asking aid and comfort in such causes, all of them unwitting testimony to the distress and confusion of mind that automatically equates schooling with education and indoctrination with learning. Eventually it seemed good to write a general answer to all such solicitations:

Guarding the
Guardians of the Guards

We have been hearing both from and about groups of citizens who have organized themselves as guardians of education and monitors of texts and techniques. Those who have written to us have praised our efforts, claiming a common cause and expecting that we will praise, and promote, their efforts. We will not. They are decent and well-meaning people disturbed about the obvious disorders of education, no doubt, but their understanding of "education" is as thoughtless and self-serving as that of the self-styled professionals of education who brought those disorders upon us.

These guardians of education, while they differ in some ways, all seem proponents of the back-to-basics frenzy, in which we find no merit. We champion mastery, and we mean mastery, not minimum competence, in language and number not because it is the goal of education but because it is absurd to imagine an educated person who lacks it. Having that mastery, we can make of knowledge the raw material of thoughtfulness and judgment. Lacking it, we can make of knowledge nothing more than the substance of training and the content of indoctrination.

The back-to-basics enthusiasts, who never fail to note the paramount importance of being able to read want-ads and to write letters of application, treat the skills of number and language as subdivisions of vocational training to be imparted and done with, as though reading a micrometer and reading a paragraph were acts of the same nature. In one sense, literacy is a trivial skill, easily acquired and neither more nor less valuable than those darlings of the schools, the "life skills," things like shoe-tying and crossing at the corner. In another sense, it is an endless and demanding enterprise that is also the ground of our knowledge and understanding, but an enterprise little likely to entice the minds of those taught literacy as a life skill.

All unwittingly, therefore, the guardians preach the same degradation of literacy that the educationists have so long practiced, and, strange as it might seem at first, for the same reason. The greatest mischief done in the schools is the attempt to inculcate certain presumed "values," but the guardians understand that less than perfectly. They fancy that the mischief lies not in the inculcation of values but in the inculcation of the educationists' values rather than the guardians' values. All would be well, they imagine, if only the school would foster the "right" values. And that is why they must make of literacy a "basic" life skill rather than a way of life. If you want to foster in children certain values and preclude others, you must take care that they do not develop an appetite for knowledge and the skill to make of it the raw material of thoughtfulness and judgment. Jefferson's words are an assertion of faith, not fact; fact may be "self-evident," but "truth" is not. If it were, earth would be fair, and all men glad and wise.

There is a momentous difference between coming to believe what we have often been told and deciding, as Jefferson did, out of knowledge and thoughtful judgment, to "hold" something true. The former is a kind of slavery and easy to achieve; the latter is difficult, for it requires knowledge and governed intellect, in other words, an education, but it is freedom.

Freedom is, to be sure, frightening. There is no telling what values free people will choose to hold. Decent and well-meaning guardians of values were horrified by the monstrous principles of the Declaration of Independence. It is, of course, out of fear that the guardians preach the inculcation of values, fear of knowledge and thought.

Most of the guardians urge things like the study of history and economics "emphasizing the benefits of the free enterprise system." We wholeheartedly share the guardians' devotion to the free enterprise system, but they obviously don't share our equal devotion to the study of history and economics, which will inevitably bring the knowledge of some facts, events, and ideas that are not at all conducive to our wholehearted devotion to the free enterprise system. When we study history from a certain point of view, we do not study history. If our students someday discover, as in fact they will, that we were sometimes mistaken in our knowledge of history, they will probably forgive us. But if they discover, as in fact they do, that we have misrepresented or omitted knowledge in the service of some values, they will learn to distrust both us and those values, as indeed they should — and apparently do.

If our values are grounded, as we usually imagine they are, in evidence and reason, then those who can see the evidence and who know the ways of reason are likely to adopt them. However, if we find ourselves tampering with the evidence and tempering the power of language, the medium of reason, then perhaps we ought to reevaluate our values. Should that prove unacceptable, we should at least be able to see that our interest would be best served not by asking the state to promulgate our values but by forbidding the state to promulgate any values at all. If the state can espouse some value that we love, it can, with equal justice, espouse others that we do not love.

The guardians do differ in one important way from the educationists. The guardians have lost their nerve, while the educationists still have plenty. The guardians, although they often wave the flag, do not truly hold the most basic value of a free society: the belief that, given the choice, knowing and thoughtful people will choose to continue in a free society. Those who do hold that value must guard against the guardians. But not in the classroom.

 ————————————————————————

We misunderstand the dangers of schooling. We fancy that what is at stake is some obviously needed widespread level of competence and ability, a large population of people able to cope with the demands of a complicated and technical system. And there is, to be sure, some danger that we will have fewer effective people than we need. But we have at stake in the schools something far more important than that, for what is effectively precluded by the essential and pervasive ideology of the government school system is nothing less than individual freedom.

We could probably say many things about the unhappy schoolboy who knows the value of a ticket and even that "people die every three second," but of them all the most important is that he is not free. His beliefs and values are not his; he is theirs. He is possessed, as anyone must be possessed who knows nothing of the claim that all things make on our thinking attention and who lacks in any case the perfectly learnable powers and skills of thinking attention. Which is to say that that schoolboy, in company with countless millions of other Americans, is held captive by illiteracy, and that we have in effect voted in favor of Proposition 3, which requires that the ignorant must be unfree if civilization is to endure. But Jefferson warned us that that might happen. What he did not foresee, unfortunately, was that we would find a way to make it happen.

Literacy is not a skill or a collection of skills, although it surely does provide many ever-growing skills; it is rather a way of the mind, the *individual* mind, for there is no other, the habit of thinking attention paid in language in the search for understanding. It is the only guarantee of freedom and the essential attribute of knowing and thoughtful people who can choose. For free people, basic minimum competency won't do, and that our schools now propose that shabby substitute for literacy is clear evidence that their collectivist ideology has nothing to do with the goal of the freedom of the individual.

A government institution serves the aims of government. The aims of even the best government, as Jefferson warned us, are *not* the same as the aims of free individuals nor can they be. Free individuals, capable of thoughtful discretion, are the necessary check to the natural propensities of what

Jefferson so aptly named the "functionaries" of government. It must follow, therefore, that if education provides us with free individuals, it is *not* in the interest of government functionaries to provide education. They must provide something else, but they must *call* it "education." In this respect, no government is different from any other, and in the following article *The Underground Grammarian* explored a frightening parallel:

The Answering of Kautski

Why should we bother to reply to Kautski? He would reply to us, and we would have to reply to his reply. There's no end to that. It will be quite enough for us to announce that Kautski is a traitor to the working class, and everyone will understand everything.

V. I. Lenin

Tyranny is always and everywhere the same, while freedom is always various. The well and truly enslaved are dependable; we know what they will say and think and do. The free are quirky. Tyrannies may be overt and violent or covert and insidious, but they all require the same thing, a subject population in which the power of thought is occluded and the power of deed brought low. That's why Lenin's bolshevism and American educationism have so much in common.

"Give me four years to teach the children," said Lenin, "and the seed I have sown will never be uprooted." He wasn't talking about reading, writing, and arithmetic. He wanted only enough of such skills so that the workers could puzzle out their quotas and so that a housebroken bureaucracy could get on with the business of rural electrification. Our educationists call it Basic Minimum Competency, and they hope that we'll settle for it as soon as they can cook up some way of convincing us that they can provide it. For Lenin, as for our educationists, to "teach the children" is to "adjust" them into some ideology.

Lenin understood the power of that ready refuge from logical thought that is called in our schools the "affective domain," the amiable Never-never Land of the half-baked, to whom anything they name "humanistic" is permitted, and of whom skillful scholarship and large knowledge are not required. Lenin approved the "teaching" of values and the display, with appropriate captions, of socially acceptable "role models." He knew all too well the worth of behavior modification. He knew that indoctrination in "citizenship" is safer than the study of history, and that a familiarity with literature is not conducive to the whole-hearted pursuit of career objectives in the real-life situation, or arena.

On the other hand, Lenin knew that there was little risk that coherent thought would erupt in minds besieged by endless prattle about the clarification of values. He knew that reiterated slogans can dull even a good mind into a stupor out of which it will never arise to overthrow the slogan-makers. In this, our educationists have followed him assiduously, justifying every new crime against freedom of language and thought by mouthing empty slogans about "quality education."

"Most of the people," Lenin wrote, not in public, of course, but in a letter, "just aren't capable of thinking. The best they can do is learn the words." If that reminds you of those bleating sheep in *Animal Farm,* try to forget them, and think instead of the lowing herds of pitiable teacher-trainees, many of whom began with good intentions and even with brains, singing for their certificates dull dirges of interpersonal interaction outcomes enhancement and of change agent skills developed in time-action line. Lenin's contempt was reserved for the masses. These educationists, pretenders to egalitarianism, hold even their own students in contempt, offering them nothing but words.

If you think it too rash to charge our educationists even as unwitting agents of tyranny and thought control, consider these lines from a recent proclamation of the Association of California School Administrators:

> "Parent choice" proceeds from the belief that the purpose of education is to provide individual students with an education. In fact, educating the individual is but a means to the true end of education, which is to create a viable social order to which individuals contribute and by which they are sustained. "Family choice" is, therefore, basically selfish and anti-social in that it focuses on the "wants" of a single family rather than the "needs" of society.

So what do you think? Would it suit Lenin?

And if you'd like to object, you'll see that these people also know how to answer Kautski. They'll just pronounce you an elitist, and everybody will understand everything.

 ———————————————————————

Thoughtful people will discover some reservations about the voucher system, against which the California administrators direct their strange homily. It does assume, contrary to evidence, that the ordinary American parent knows what an education is and prizes it, and it will provide lucrative opportunities for even more fools and charlatans than the schools now harbor. In fact, the best thing that can be said for the voucher system is that it clearly terrifies the educationists and drives them to admit, out of a mindless frenzy, apparently, for the admission is most damning, that "educating the individual is but a means to the *true* end of education, which is to create a viable social order to which individuals contribute and by which they are sustained." They almost certainly say exactly the same thing in the schools of Albania.

It was the American promise that free individuals would be more important than any "social order," and that it was for them to choose how best *it* might be formed and sustained. Nor is it suggested in the Declaration of Independence that the individual's pursuit of his "wants" is "basically selfish and anti-social" and antithetical to the "needs" of the society. But then the chances are very good that no member of the Association of California School Administrators has pondered the meanings of the Declaration of Independence. Indeed, as inheritors of the ideology of *Cardinal Principles*, the California principals have probably never so much as read it, since "civics should concern itself less with constitutional questions and remote governmental functions, and should direct attention to social agencies close at hand and to the informal activities of daily life that regard and seek the common good."

The common good. How splendid that sounds. But when William Blake once gave his thinking attention to the perennial cry of those who justified their deeds in the name of the common good, he had to conclude:

He who would do good to another must do it in Minute Particulars. General Good is the plea of the scoundrel, hypocrite, flatterer; for Art and Science cannot exist but in minutely organized Particulars.

The deepest, most pervasive theme of American educationism is the rejection of minutely organized particulars for the sake of vaguely appreciated generalities. If the former are the substance of Art and Science, of what are the latter the substance?

I can't think of any pat answer to that question, but I cannot help believing that those whose minds wander in the work of vaguely appreciated generalities and who cannot give themselves to the organization of minute particulars cannot in any sense be free, and may not, in some special sense, be fully human. If the direction of thinking attention to the claim of events and facts is the essentially human act, performed in the essentially human medium of language, what can we say of those who are unable to perform that act, but that they are unfree in a state of civilization?

Rousseau had it backward. We are *not* born free. We are born in the chains of the random and reflexive, and are ignorant and unreasonable by simple nature. We must learn to be free, to organize the random and detect the reflexive, to acquire the knowledge of particulars and the powers of reason. The examined life is impossible if we cannot examine, order, classify, define, distinguish, always in minute particulars. It was a premise of the founders of American educationism that what they called "ethical character" could be instilled, indeed, might *better* be instilled, without attention to intellectual discipline. Out of that premise they devised their "affective domain" and set it over against the merely "cognitive domain" as a somewhat *more* than equal and independent principality, where they might wander comfortably among the unmeasurables, the feelings and sentiments and values and "worthy emotional responses." Of that affective domain I must now say four things, which, although I have to put them in some order, are equally important:

1. It is out of resort to the affective domain that educationists can palm off as "education" everything from folk

dancing to bulletin board decoration and visits to nursing homes, and, at the same time, so neglect the merely cognitive disciplines that they can spend twelve whole years in the teaching of something as simple as conventional punctuation and still fail to teach it.

2. The affective domain is a logical absurdity. Feelings, sentiments, values, and responses have causes, attributes, and consequences. We can *know* nothing of them, we can neither understand nor judge them, without the work of the intellect in the organization of minute particulars. You may call "affective" whatever you please, but you cannot deal with it unless you are cognitive.

3. The feelings, sentiments, values, and responses of our children, or of any citizens, are none of the government's damned business. That we must support a government agency that gives itself to the emotional and ideological manipulation of citizens is infamous. That it should, out of that intrusive manipulation, provide us with who can say how many young citizens who cannot think coherently but who do "appreciate" the value of a fifteen-dollar ticket to a rock concert is an unspeakable outrage.

4. It is the supposed existence and paramountcy of the affective domain that have made the teachers' colleges what they are, nurseries of self-indulgence, unskilled "creativity," and half-baked pseudo-metaphysical incantation. Silly as it may seem, training in the efficient storage of chalk and erasers would actually be of more value to the incipient schoolteacher than a whole experiential continuum of intercultural awareness-enhancement, but if teacher-training were devoted only to the cognitive it could be very quickly accomplished by very few people. The professionals of edu-

cation can justify their continued employment in great numbers only if they can convince us that they alone can initiate supplicants into the mysteries. It is only in the cognitive domain, which they scorn, that charlatanism is readily unmasked.

Nevertheless, and although the colonists could hardly have been more oppressed by the king than we are by the schools, there seems to be no hope of a Declaration of Independence, to say nothing of a revolution. This time, the people, already massively indoctrinated by the values teaching of the schools, are willing parties to their own oppression. We *want* the schools to teach values, and we *believe* what they have told us, that concrete knowledge and strict intellectual discipline are not only separate from "ethical character" but perhaps actually impediments to that lofty goal.

The makers of *Cardinal Principles* were true prophets when they said that, where the formation of "ethical character" was intended, the school was "the one agency that [could] be controlled definitely and consciously." And they did it. The national "ethical character," whatever it may be, didn't just happen; it is the result of definite and conscious control. Nor can we free ourselves from that control, not only accepted but even approved by most Americans, without an enormous change in many millions of individual minds. Such a change could be wrought only through universal public education, which is exactly what we do not have. We have universal public *schooling*, which is not even close to education. The confusion between schooling and education, which suffuses every one of the Seven Deadly Principles, and out of which the principle-makers did their work, is what the schools have by now taught us all. It is their only triumph, the only lesson they have taught universally and with complete effectiveness; but it is enough. It took them a bit more than four years, to be sure, but they do seem to have planted a seed that can never be uprooted. Lenin would be envious.

Afterword:
Plus Ça Change

As I was approaching what I hoped would be the end of this book, I received a fat manila envelope from a high-ranking staff officer in the educationistic bureaucracy of the State of New York. His letter, clipped to a great wad of that slick and grimy-looking paper that comes out of copying machines covered with that medium gray print that always makes you want to polish your glasses, read:

> Your advice and example are among the influences on the attached grant proposal to the National Endowment for the Humanities for "A Program of Renew Education in Basic Humanities Disciplines." Because of your influence, I thought you ought to get a copy of the proposal while we are still awaiting the results of NEH's peer review, which we should have in March and April. I would like to hear your reaction to the proposal (which, you will note, includes a field-test in New Jersey), and I hope that we will be able to call on you for advice on the project if it is funded. Please don't hesitate to write or call me with questions or advice.

Although the writer was not unknown to me, and although I had actually once spent a day nattering about this and that at the headquarters of his vast bureaucracy, I could think of no way to justify calling that "advice and example," to say nothing of "influence." Furthermore, I felt vaguely discomfited to be even a putative party to that process in which one educationistic bureaucracy solicits a slice of our money from another educationistic bureaucracy in order to remedy some newly visible deficiency caused by a third educationistic bureaucracy. If the teacher-training academies of America had not devoted themselves for more than half a century to militant anti-intellectualism, there would now be no need for the National Endowment for the Humanities to take some of our money and give it to the New York State Department of Education, which will thereupon set about beginning to start to prepare to do what it damn well ought to have been doing all along. Accordingly, in spite of my correspondent's advice not to hesitate with questions or advice, I hesitated.

As I hesitated, it dawned on me. Of course. I was looking at the latest Great Lurch Forward. The whole history of American educationism can be told in Great Lurches Forward. When we recently noticed that even the taxpayers had noticed that astonishingly few high school graduates could read or write, we made the Great Lurch Forward into Basic Minimum Competency. Well, all right, said our educationists, *now* we know what to do. That was what they had said when we were all so dispirited by the dread Sputnik, which Clifton Fadiman reminded us, although in vain, was simply a flying dog in a metal box, but which frightened most of us enough to make us turn for succor to the educationists, probably the only people around who couldn't provide any. Aha! they said; *now* we know what to do. And they lurched forward. Since the day of the Great Primal Lurch, the lifeadjustmentism of *Cardinal Principles*, they have lurched from one bold innovative thrust to another. They have lurched out of "self-contained" classrooms right back into them, lurching in the meanwhile in and out of pods and modules. They have lurched from the old math to the new math to the balancing of checkbooks *instead* of math. And now they are going to lurch into The Humanities.

The lurchers, notably imperceptive of irony in any case, see no irony at all in proposing that those who couldn't even make us a minimally literate nation will now make us the possessors of the "thoughtful discretion" of which Jefferson dreamed. Since I *do* know something about these lurchers in Albany who claim my influence, I can testify that they are not cynical opportunists booking themselves cushy berths on the next great lurch, but that is no consolation. In fact, I could wish they *were* cynical opportunists, for it may well be that the false and mercenary preacher will convert, out of well-pretended zeal, more souls than will ever be moved by decent, ineffectual honesty. And the Albany lurchers, surely decent and honest, will just as surely prove ineffectual.

Like all those who imagine that it is possible to change or reform the government education system, they seem to have a mistaken metaphor in their heads. I think they see "the schools" as an apparatus of some sort, even, as many educationists unhappily call it, a "delivery system," something like UPS. There are the trucks. They exist. They even run. You can put in them and then deliver anything you choose. All we have to do is choose. If we choose some nice humanities, we'll deliver them. But government education is not a neutral vessel into which and out of which diverse fluids can be poured. It is not even an apparatus that can be set or programmed to do whatever we want of it. It is more like an elaborate and complicated organism that has inevitably evolved into exactly and only the creature that can do exactly and only what it must do to survive. It is even more like an extensive, interlocking ecosystem, something like the Great Dismal Swamp, in which every plant and creature, and even the air and earth and water, are what they are and do what they do because that's the way it must be. You can shoot the tiger, or you can stay out of his way, but you cannot pronounce him a vegetarian.

Here is just one of the objectives of the "Language Arts/ English Syllabi" as put forth in the proposal from the New York State Education Department, already tainted, you probably noticed, by that slash, which reveals that no one has paid any thoughtful attention to the conjunction, and thus to the *exact* nature of the relationship, between those hokey Language Arts, already infamous, and mere English:

> Instruction in critical thinking will be integrated into the classroom activities of reading, discussion, and writing about literature and other writing of recognized high quality. The complexity and difficulty of the reading, writing, and discussion will increase progressively from kindergarten through grade twelve.

That certainly sounds great. But, for anyone who knows something of what is done in our schools and teacher academies, who has seen how the work of the mind is done by the theoreticians who design programs, who has an inkling of how education is governed and directed, some questions arise. Who will provide all that instruction in critical thinking? Will they be the teachers who have themselves been exhaustively trained in values clarification and in relating? Will those who carried signs promoting "Quality Educacion" and "Descent Wages for Teachers" cast light on "literature and other writing of recognized high quality"? Will the assistant superintendent for instruction, the ex-shop teacher with a small real estate business on the side, devise the parameters of the plan to integrate the instruction in critical thinking into the various classroom activities? Will that instruction be also integrated into the making of collages for the bulletin board and the appreciation of other cultures at the Christmas party featuring the cookies of many lands? Who will decide, and how, exactly what "complexity" is suitable for the fourth grade and what for the sixth? An ex-guidance counselor turned principal? An ex-principal turned coordinator in Albany? Will the publishers and legislators and professors of education disband their Triple Entente and leave the choice of "literature and other writing of recognized high quality" to the critically thinking teachers? Will the parents, themselves unthinking products of long years of values indoctrination and helpless against the random suggestions of any and all indoctrinators, be tickled pink when their children bring all that critical thinking home? And you can probably devise for yourself dozens of other depressing questions about what is in fact one tiny entry in thirty single-spaced pages of similar "objectives" and schemes and devices.

Furthermore, we can see that in the schools history becomes social studies, writing becomes a communication skill, literature becomes propaganda, and even science becomes brushing after meals. What will "humanities" become? I am sad to say that I have a clue, for in my own school I have seen recently a supposed attempt to cash in on the next Great Lurch Forward, which, fortunately, failed. I say "fortunately" because had it succeeded we would in fact have been further than ever from the education of "informed discretion."

To see why that failure was fortunate, you must first know some generally hidden things about a public college. By "humanities," for instance, we mean those studies that do not lead to clearly identifiable paying jobs, and in fact we hardly ever use the word except when we have to distinguish those few and antique disciplines from such things as teacher-training or business education, which are the *routine* enterprises of the college. Furthermore, we *never* speak of "the liberal arts"; we are prevented by a superstitious dread of the kind that would prevent the surviving peasants from uttering aloud the name of Count Dracula. When we do have to admit that all our students ought to share some body of knowledge, and can thus be passed off as members in good standing of Western Culture, we call that what almost every other school in America calls it — "general education." General education, of course, is to education exactly what general science is to science, a smattering of this and that. Nor is "general education" a euphemism for the liberal arts, and certainly not for the humanities. It is, in fact, not an intellectual entity but a political device, the result of a reluctant compromise among the teachers of everything from puppet-making to self-awareness through massage. It has neither center nor theme, and everyone, although for purely sectarian reasons, agrees that it is simply a mess.

One of our subcommittees undertook to reform general education. After many months of arduous labor, the subcommittee brought forth — well, certainly not a mouse, but something more like a hydra as big as the Ritz — a hydra as it might be designed by a subcommittee, however. Its details were only mildly interesting, but its theme was fascinating.

It derived all of its recommendations from something that you will recognize: the Student Outcomes Principle. It began by saying, and said again and again throughout, that the "aims" of courses of study were certain student outcomes, which might well be achieved — which, indeed, might *best* be achieved — not by any traditionally practiced studies but by the ad hoc invention of innovative interdisciplinary studies and other gimmicks.

One of the desired student outcomes, for instance, was "an appreciation of the role of science and technology in the modern world." (Yes, "appreciation." *Plus ça change.*) While the proposal did concede that such an appreciation might have something to do with "a course *oriented toward* [my italics, and well merited, too] the discipline of physics, chemistry, biology, geology, or astronomy," it quite specifically and emphatically rejected the quaint and elitist notion that a student ought to take a basic *course* in one of those disciplines. Such a course is neither innovative nor interdisciplinary and cannot be expected, therefore, to provide that appreciation which is the desirable student outcome. Furthermore, a basic course in some hard science provides no opening at all for some nervous member of a shrinking education department who is also a skillful tinkerer with automobiles and motorcycles and who could surely, as teacher-trainee enrollments decline, impart in a real-life situation a worthy appreciation of the role of science and technology in the modern world. (Since I myself do all the typesetting and printing for *The Underground Grammarian*, I suggested that I too might teach a course in the appreciation of science and technology. My printing press itself exemplifies all of the cunning embodiments of the principles of mechanics that made the Industrial Revolution, and *every single one* of Newton's famous, but now unknown, Laws of Motion can be seen at work in that machine. And appreciated. The subcommittee members nodded emphatically, pleased to see that a notorious slow learner was coming around. You cannot, in fact, dream up anything so preposterous that you will not find it being taught in some school.)

The "humanities" are not mentioned in the proposal, although "the human environment" is. And there are the "integrative studies," in which "innovation and experimentation are strongly encouraged," and which ought to include things like Racism, Sexism in the United States Today, or New Directions in the Search for Meaning. For obvious reasons, the study of foreign languages is *not* to be considered a necessary part of every student's general education, although there would be little harm in teaching a student to appreciate the fact that there are foreign languages. In every respect, even in its call for a massive new bureaucracy to serve the needs of general education, the proposal derives directly from the ideology, and often even from the very text, of *Cardinal Principles.*

That's ominous, because there couldn't have been more than two or three members of that subcommittee who had ever even *heard* of *Cardinal Principles.* Indeed, some of those members are so clearly devoted to things like intellectual discipline and all that mere information that they would recoil in dismay from a clear statement of the ideology of *Cardinal Principles.* This must mean that that ideology has so thoroughly seeped into American schooling at every level that it has become the ground of who can say how many rarely noticed and therefore rarely examined assumptions. Those assumptions are dangerous, and there can never be the education that Jefferson intended while they are the daily food and drink of the schools. And they are. Even the academically disciplined members of the subcommittee signed their names (what were they thinking? *were* they thinking?) to this:

> The realization that study areas refer to desirable outcomes and that these may be met in a variety of ways, ways that may at times deny the custom-established claims to coveted provinces of instruction, broadens the possibilities of curricular offerings immeasurably.

The ideologues of educationism (fortunately for us, if we will pay thoughtful attention) have so thoroughly given themselves to their disdain of intellectual discipline that they *always*, and always inadvertently, reveal some truth when they pretend to do the work of the mind in writing. It isn't true, as popular opinion fancies, that the unskilled writer fails to make himself clear; he is far more likely to make himself all too clear. While there is no clear meaning *in the assertion* that areas "refer to" outcomes and that outcomes can be "met," there *is* a clear meaning in the fact that the assertion is made in such a murky way. The very use of the word "realization" is a mindless twitch of longing, for in no way can the Student Outcomes Principle be put forth as some fact to be "realized" but only as an assertion to be believed. It is simply true that he who pauses to choose the right word will *find out* what he means to mean, and he who can't will make it clear to his reader that he is ignorant and thoughtless.

But the most unsettling revelation of that passage is of the automatic assumption that underlies the characterization of

the "claims of disciplines" as "custom-established" and
"provinces of instruction" as "coveted." What else must be
true of one who automatically assumes that it is out of
custom that we turn to the scholar of history for knowledge
and understanding of history? Would he also assume that it
is out of nothing more than custom that we take our shoes
to the cobbler or our teeth to the dentist? What can you
guess about devotion to discipline and the love of learning
in one who airily presumes that it is out of *covetousness* that
the physicists greedily demand the privilege of teaching the
physics courses? When the outcome seeker suggests that we
might do better to teach the appreciation of history and
physics by devising innovative interdisciplinary courses to
replace the customary and coveted work of the physicists
and historians, who is covetous? Such bizarre notions are
not only possible but inevitable in a world where there really
are no academic disciplines, where this year's general science
teacher may just as well be next year's guidance counselor
and then another year's assistant principal for instruction,
where this year's professor of curriculum facilitation will
probably be next year's grants proposal coordinator and another year's supervisor of pre-service hands-on experiential
continua. Among the educationists, who make policy and
devise theory, there is so little experience of academic discipline that they probably really *can't* imagine any reason
other than "custom" for giving the teaching of physics into
the hands of the physicists. Physics, for them, is not a concrete and complicated body of real knowledge and understanding but just one of many vaguely similar vehicles for
the enhancement of appreciation. Nor is it surprising that
those who have, because the mere teaching of general science

or social studies did not arise from or command love and devotion, indeed coveted the nobler and more lucrative work of the guidance counselor should imagine that the scholar of history has seized his chair, in which he seems so disturbingly and unaccountably content, out of covetousness.

What can we hope for now that such people have boldly announced their intention to devise new programs of emphasis on the great role of the humanities in the development of Western Civilization and the powers of knowledge and critical thought as the necessary virtues of a free society?

Nothing.

Or, more precisely, nothing but more of the same.

The state of American government education is simply not a "problem" that can be solved. It is rather an enormous fact of life, a self-perpetuating institution elaborated from within by principle, not caprice, governed by collective assent, not individual talent. It easily absorbs the shock of every criticism by pretending to "reform" itself, only to transform and dilute whatever it claims to embrace into nothing but more of the same. It easily swallows and digests and incorporates into its substance everything in the world around it, popular fads and fancies just as readily as appropriately diluted new knowledge in genetics or psychology or in any of the disciplines that it will not teach. Whatever there is in our society — fast-food merchandizing, militant homosexualism, disco dancing, supply-side economics, weird religious cultism, futurology through computers, jogging, astrology, est, you name it — will find its analogue in the schools.

The Commission for the Reorganization of Secondary Education set out to adjust the ordinary American child, whatever that might be, to life in American society, whatever *that* might be. It did not clearly and fully understand either, but who does? It nevertheless succeeded prodigiously, if only by a roundabout way. By now the children — and the children of the children of those children — whom they "adjusted" have *become* American society. In strictest truth, therefore, it may *not* be correct to say that the educational system absorbs and replicates the mindless fads and the manipulative practices of society and commerce. It may be just the other way around. After more than half a century of preparing children for life, our government education system has prepared a life for children.

That system is a tiger that we can neither kill nor evade. To shoot the tiger is unthinkable; the consequent social and economic upheaval would turn us from a nation of children into a nation of crazy and desperate children, a condition from which we are now (more or less) protected not by the good offices of the schools but by their mere existence as employers and purchasers of goods and services. Furthermore, the ideologues and leaders of teachers' unions are indisputably correct when they recite, to the thunderous applause of millions of government employees, the assertion that a free society is impossible without a free, public, and universal system of education, although they are absolutely wrong in imagining that an *education* is what that system in fact provides. Curiously enough, therefore, that assertion is actually an incitement to the abolition of the public school system, for we will never find that universal education, which we do in very fact require in a free society, in these schools.

If we *do* want to "do something" about the schools, we

must begin by giving up forever the futile hope that the educationists will do it for us if only we ask them often enough. Governmental agencies do not change from within except for their own purposes, and their "responses" to external cries for change, even when well meant, are inevitably subterfuges. However, while public education is best understood as simply another government agency, it does differ from the IRS and the Marine Corps in one supremely important detail: it harbors hosts of dissidents, dissidents who are themselves sick to death of what they see in the system that demeans and subverts their best efforts. The plight of dissidents in the soviet of educationism embodies precisely the principal thematic tension that engendered *Cardinal Principles*: They are individual minds and talents caught in a system of collective ideologies and values.

Consider, for instance, the case of a certain tenth-grade English teacher in a Maryland high school. This audacious fellow had his students read the *Poetics* of Aristotle and *The Prince* of Machiavelli as obviously useful and thought-provoking adjuncts to the study of *Julius Caesar*. Since Aristotle and Machiavelli are not approved by the local curriculum facilitators, the teacher, who refused to recant, was suspended without pay for insubordination and misconduct in office. (At this writing, he is still awaiting trial, and I have no idea what will become of him.) The superintendent of the school system where this outrage occurred was quoted in *Time* (December 15, 1980) as follows:

> I don't know whether [he] is right or wrong about the books. But in a public school system, you have to have reasonable procedures to determine what is to be used, and the superintendent has to uphold them. . . . What

if a teacher decided to use *Playboy* or *Hustler*? I think the school system has an obligation to set standards and to set curriculum.

Forgive me, reader, if I fear that you may have missed the main point of this little story. If you are exasperated at yet another suggestion that we have put the yahoos in charge of the schools, then you *have* missed the main point. That superintendent, yahoo or not — and it doesn't really matter — is absolutely right. He recites with perfect accuracy the principles of an ideological collectivism. Now *you* might say, speaking as an individual mind that can know, understand, and judge, that the difference between *Playboy* and the *Poetics* is obvious. It is, quite simply, a matter of worth. But a superintendent is *not* an individual mind but rather a functionary of a collective ideology. It is *not* his function to know, understand, and judge, but only to function appropriately according to his place in the apparatus. (That sort of "worker" seems superbly characterized by the word "apparatchik," the best possible job description for most of the people who "educate" our children.) The apparatus is not intended to distinguish what is worthy from what is not, but what is *approved* from what is not. That distinction requires only knowledge of the list, and it absolutely precludes understanding and judgment. Therefore, from the point of view of the apparatus of which the superintendent is simply a component, there *is* no difference between *Playboy* and the *Poetics*. We have thus an educational system that, exactly *because* it is "values oriented," can by its intrinsic nature have no values whatsoever, but only collectively derived "standards."

Now, if you still dream that education can be changed by

the people who work in it, imagine yourself trying to discuss that little matter with that superintendent, the man in charge of the life and work of the intellect in a whole school system, and who says, "I don't know whether he is right or wrong about the books." Remember, he speaks the truth. He *doesn't* know. In that imagined conference you will see a miniature but perfectly accurate paradigm of all intentions to change the government schools.

It is instructive to notice that when dissidents are unmasked in the schools, it is usually because of a book. I mean, of course, *a book*, not a textbook. A book is the permanent record of the work of a solitary human mind, to be read, marked, learned, and inwardly digested by another solitary human mind. A committee can no more make a book than it can play the violin, but almost every "book" used in schools — and in teacher-training academies — is written collectively and for collective purposes. The makers of schoolbooks are "writers" only in the sense that the sign painter who labels bathroom doors is a "writer," or the pilot who draws in the sky slogans in smoke. Such messages — enormously dignified in schools as "communications" — can never, however long and seemingly complex they become, provide the substance of anything more than collective training. Education comes from books. And it goes into books. Education arises when one mind ponders the work of another. Thus, since the elements and circumstances of an education are beyond number, since all minds are different not only from one another but even from their earlier selves, there is no end to understanding, no final judgment. And that is why books are so scarce in schools and why a teacher can find himself a pariah in the "academic" enterprise because of an essay by Aristotle. The schools are devoted to collective conclusions, what that superintendent calls "standards," and not to the interminable (and to educationists "selfish and anti-social") ruminations of understanding and judgment.

A magnificent education, as countless examples attest, can come from nothing more than reading and writing. In the one we behold the work of the solitary mind, in the other we do it, but we do it in such a way that we can behold again, and understand, and judge, the work of a solitary mind — our own. In the cause of education, there are no substitutes for reading and writing, nor do they require any supplements. Film-strips and flip-charts and all the countless gimmicks and gadgets that clutter our classrooms — which are, by the way, every bit as profitable as the antennas and jet exhaust fumes so righteously deplored by our humanisticist educationists — are the trash and pollution of education and reveal the schools' corporate belief that children are mentally crippled and must be cajoled into learning anything at all. But the gimmickry of the schools is more than simple cajolery, which most students see quite clearly as something between condescension and contempt; it is an integral and large portion of a general program designed to prevent solitude. And while the children themselves are pestered with values clarification modules and relating sessions and group activities lest they fall into solitude, they are also protected from dangerous exposure to the fruits of solitary thinking in others. Committees and commissions and teaching teams and curriculum standard setters make the film-strips and movies and tapes and slide-shows and packets of learning materials. Their very teachers, raised in the same tradition and then doubly indoctrinated in the teacher-training academies, are not solitary minds but collective spokesmen, not minds that pursue understanding but only mouths that transmit communications. The system will find no fault in any teacher, no matter how scant his knowledge, who is ever mindful of awareness enhancement and the parameters of remediational strategies in meeting the felt needs of the whole child, but it will suspend without pay a teacher who brings into class a nonstandard work of a solitary mind.

Still, some dissidents do survive. And, because they are themselves solitary minds, some few lucky students will find, even in the worst school, the beginnings of an education. The dissidents are those teachers we all remember, the Miss Morrisons and the Mr. Martins who made — we don't know just how — some important difference. And they will always make that important difference, although our schools of education make it harder and harder for a solitary mind to emerge intact and independent. But they will save only a few other solitary minds here and there. They cannot save, or reform, or even change the system. Two facts prevent them: They are almost always *teachers*, privates in the ranks, the least powerful and influential people in the schools; and, for all the good that they do now and then, their self-interest is best served by the same establishment that harbors and rewards the guidance counselors and curriculum facilitators and the supervisors and superintendents and all the whole host of fools and frauds who could probably not make a living in anything other than a government agency. They are — the dissidents — also government agents.

We have reached a point at which even Mencken's sound advice would be no help. Sure, we could probably burn down all the colleges and hang all the professors, but that would still leave us with fifty state departments of education, and a federal one, hundreds of educationistic research institutes and curriculum development outfits, a like number of publishers and learning materials designers and manufacturers, who knows how many awareness-orientated teachers' centers, and who can count what else, including the National Education Association and the American Federation of Teachers. Unfortunately, burning the colleges and hanging the professors just won't do it. Our schools, a parody of education, are impervious to anything less than revolution — obliteration and reconstitution. But that is impossible.

In the first place, nobody cares that much. It just isn't worth the trouble. The only ones who care, although not *that* much, might be the dissidents, but they can never make a revolution. In America we have rules for revolution, and obviously good rules at that. Who would make a revolution among us is expected to pledge thereto life, fortune, and sacred honor. Some of us dissidents (I think I can speak for them) would like no doubt to imagine pledging our lives in some great cause, but when you get right down to it there is nothing more at stake here than the freedom of somebody else's children. Besides, we have contracts. Whether we can pledge our lives or not they do not specify, but they do make it clear that there is to be no tampering with the terms and conditions of our employment. As to our fortunes, well, you know very well that we have none. Most unaccountably, the wise and happy society of ethical characters and worthy citizens that we have fostered for so long in our schools now seems to value us less than it values bus drivers and trash collectors. So we can pledge no fortunes, not even our guaranteed annual increments. And as to that sacred honor, which sounds suspiciously antiquated and elitist, you do have to admit that it is a value notoriously difficult to clarify in group discussions. On that we must pass. The closest we might come is to pledge our tenure, but we can't. It sounds noble, of course, but it would simply erode the standards of the profession.

But maybe things will change.

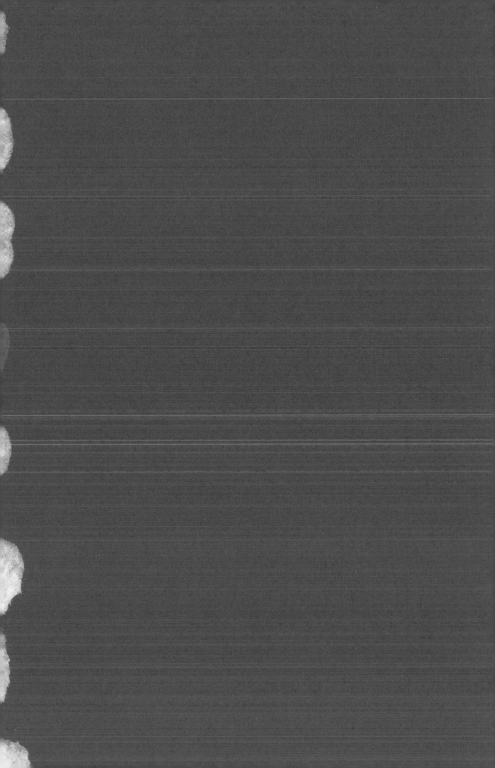